MAGIC NIGHTS

A Treasure Map and Travel Guide
to the Ocean of Power and Possibility
in Your Sleeping Mind

KATIE HAWN, DC

The Divine Creatives Group, LLC

First printing 2011

SEL013000
Self-Help / Personal Growth / General

ISBN 978-0-615-44212-9

Library of Congress Control Number: 2011923164

Published by The Divine Creatives Group, LLC

PO Box 315
Lambertville, New Jersey 08530

Cover Art by Armor Keller
Cover design by Daniel Yeager | Nu-Image Design, April B. White and John Miller
Layout design by Daniel Yeager | Nu-Image Design

I acknowledge and offer my deepest heartfelt gratitude

to all my friends, helpers, healers, teachers and guides

who have led me to this place of unveiling.

It is my fondest wish that all of our souls' brightest gifts

will shine with this work and all works of love

now and in all days to come.

TABLE OF CONTENTS

YOU ARE THE TREASURE YOU SEEK

YOUR INNER WISDOM IS YOUR BEST GUIDANCE

YOUR IMMUNE SYSTEM IS YOUR BEST DEFENSE

THE UNIVERSE IS YOUR BEST FRIEND

ALL YOU HAVE TO DO IS BELIEVE IT

LUCKILY, WE ARE ALL WAITING HERE FOR YOU

JUST BEYOND YOUR DREAMS

EVERY MAGIC NIGHT

A TRAVEL BROCHURE

INTRODUCING THE ADVENTURE

Nighttime is when we sleep. We lay down to rest because our bodies require it to survive. Sleep too much and we seem to be sleeping our life away. Sleep too little and we just can't function when we are awake. If we don't sleep at all, we eventually go insane.

We dream, or don't dream. We wake up rested, or we just wake up because we must face the day ahead, like it or not. A full third of our lives is spent in sleep. Is a time of rest, as necessary as it is, all we are going to get, or can there be more? Science is just beginning to see that we can learn during our sleep. And dreams have always been the stuff of psychological examination. But this is just the tip of the iceberg of our potential. Like the early explorers braving the ocean waters in search of new worlds, we in our sleep and dreaming time can explore our own inner ocean, which is overflowing with more potential and possibility than we can imagine.

When we go to sleep it's like traveling to another world, like floating out to sea in a little boat, not exactly sure what lies beyond the horizon. Most of us are comfortable pushing the boat out from shore just a little, hoping to drift peacefully, so that when we awaken in the morning, we will feel refreshed and ready for the new day.

Most of us also have had some experiences with dreams and visions that defy our ability to explain. There is that sneaking suspicion that there is more out on that ocean, and perhaps beyond that peaceful horizon, than we know. After all, how much of our brain do we really use consciously? Ten percent? How much do we really know about the universe, or is it the multiverse? Much less than that.

Just imagine that when you sleep you could go to a place where you can solve problems, heal or just get a little further toward peace, joy and purpose in your life. You could find answers to all those questions that go around and around in your mind: How can I get rich? How can I get that dream job? How can I wake up a little better, a little clearer, a little healthier? How can I get things done when I am asleep? How can I learn something new or remember something I seem to have forgotten? How can I evolve into a new attitude that will help me move forward in my life?

Then there are the bigger questions that you might find yourself asking: What is really best for me anyway? Who would I be if all my life's challenges and burdens were suddenly released? What would it feel like to be my Authentic Self? Who, out there in the vast universe, can help me with all of this?

Since scientists estimate that we use only about ten percent of our brain at any given time, what is this "unused" part of our brain capable of? Is it waiting up there in our heads for us to decide to go exploring among its vast networks of neurons and to finally discover how to use it in its full capacity?

2

In New Age philosophy, it is said that a mere three percent of our be-ing, our complete soul and self, is actually located inside our physical bodies. The larger version of our be-ing knows the truth of our full power and potential, and about the real power and potential in the universe around us and in us. And what of this universe? How much do we really understand about it? How much knowledge and wisdom is out there waiting patiently to be recognized for what it is?

This guidebook will help you tap into some of these vast resources using the creative and imaginative part of your brain in a more expansive and adventurous way. It's more than saying "Now I lay me down to sleep ..." It's knowing that we all can reach further and higher. It's knowing that the power of our own mind and our own soul is so much more than we have been taught. It's knowing that these are truly wonderful and magical times full of potential. There are many lands and levels of awareness and wonderful treasures out in that vast ocean of the universe within and without. And there is always a hand reaching out, inviting us to explore these places and helping us to be the truly powerful creators we are meant to be.

Historically, people who meditated and received help from the great beyond (or perhaps the great within) were called saints, mystics, prophets or shamans. Today in this age of science, quantum physics and virtual reality, we all know there are powerful forces at work all around us that we are simply unable to see with our eyes or feel with our hands. And we are just beginning to get comfortable tapping into these powers to help us in our daily lives. People who regularly use hypnosis, meditate, do yoga and are following their intuition do so without fear of being branded as witches. It is now a well known fact that these practices are beneficial to the health of our minds and bodies.

3

Just as there are yoga classes and styles to suit every age and body type, the style of intention and meditation that is described in Magic Nights can be customized to reflect your particular lifestyle, talents and goals. You don't have to be psychic or know how to meditate. All it takes is a little time, a little *in*tention and a little *at*tention.

Just plan fifteen minutes a day of quiet time to focus on your goals; five minutes at night to set your intention and ten minutes in the morning to pay attention. Then pay attention during the day to your gut feelings, your intuition and any inspirations that may come along. And prepare to be pleasantly surprised at what life brings you.

How to Use This Book

While you are reading my Captain's Logbook and tales of adventure, I invite you to try the experience of a Magic Nights journey. Just look for these treasure maps throughout the book First, start your own Captain's Logbook by thinking deep thoughts before you sleep, or with a journal and pen in hand during the day. Then I will be your Co-Captain and take you out onto my Magic Nights ship for a few journeys. I have also included some fun day-time shore excursions along the way to help you move toward your goals.

The text of Magic Nights will give deeper understanding and more examples. It will also show why the words I have given and the ways of asking are a good way to begin your own journeys. As a help, there is a not-so-secret code: throughout this book *the Magic Words will be in italics.*

Though my personal style is visually and spiritually adventurous; an inner world and dream world that is frequently a grand theatrical production with many colorful characters, this technique is designed to be completely customizable to your personal style and needs. When you understand the basic guidelines, you can create your own ship in the way that feels most perfect for you and takes advantage of your unique tastes, talents and abilities. It could be a sleek, high tech speed boat or a crystalline space ship or an old fashioned pirate-style ship or a minimalist Zen-like oceangoing vessel. Choose your Magic Nights ship, try on a few captain's hats, peruse the travel brochure and have fun!

THE SHIP'S SAFETY MANUAL

When getting ready for any adventure, it's important to be prepared. You need the right travel papers, a travel agent, a guidebook, and an itinerary. Also it's smart to take some safety precautions such as having travel insurance as well as experienced guides and guards during your trip and a first aid kit close at hand.

Before I give you the magic words to set sail, I want to offer you every advantage of my experience in the lands of the unseen. I also want to give you effective tools and rules that will keep your journey as safe and productive as possible. The safety rules are not difficult or time consuming, but they are important, like looking both ways before crossing a street. Further along, as you become more experienced, you might break some of the rules, and find tools of your own. But it's important to know the rules and how to use the tools and why they are there before going it alone. The further you go, and the more exotic and daring the trip, the more preparation and understanding you will need.

I recently traveled across the great deserts of Egypt for two weeks while on a wonderful guided tour. It was the perfect answer to the emotional stress of losing my mother to cancer. Her illness was short, but an intense experience for me. When she passed, I wanted to do something big and different to shift my energy. I wanted to reboot, to press a reset button for my life. I was motivated. And the universe provided.

I had a new friend who had a wonderful habit of going on trips to exotic places with spiritually minded groups. She was about to go to Peru and urged me to join her tour. The trip seemed too soon and that destination didn't resonate with who I was and what I needed. But the same spiritual group would be traveling through Egypt in a few months. I had always dreamed of what it would be like to go to Egypt, and the timing was perfect.

I realized that I had just enough money to do something wild, I had a little time, and the trip presented itself to me on a silver platter. It was one of those moments where I knew that if I didn't go on this trip I would regret it for the rest of my life. And I couldn't find a reasonable reason not to go. It was with people who were like me, seeking more than just to see and touch that ancient exotic land. These people were ready for transformation and were sensitive to the energies of things in the same way that I was. So I set my sights on those hot sands and old temples and began to make all the arrangements.

Still I needed to be sure of my safety - on all levels. I knew that as much adventure and magic that I would find, there would also be unique challenges. I was going to Egypt to discover and experience more light, but I also knew that I had to be aware and awake to any shadows that might accompany it.

Choosing the right tour guide, reading the right books and traveling with a group of people that had integrity ensured that despite the language and cultural differences we would be safe and well cared for. Sometimes this safety came in the form of armed escorts for our bus and while walking around the towns and cities. The phrase "riding shotgun" came alive for me when I saw our guard "riding machine gun" in the front of our bus. We were seldom left to wander about on our own, and fortunately our adventure was rewarding and fun and without incident.

For those of us who are sensitive, energetic and spiritual, safety was also necessary. Although we call ourselves light workers, there are among us moths, attracted to our flames. And they are typically completely unaware of the challenges they present. During the trip, those of us so challenged did our best to neutralize this "moth" energy in others. We knew that judging one of us would cast a shadow on all of our essential humanity and value, and would deny us the opportunity for our souls' growth in this life.

Everyone in every aspect of life runs into moth people who just drive them crazy or "push their buttons." These button pushers may affect some people strongly and others not at all. Sometimes these button pushers can be quite powerful in their effect and we have to be prepared for them. Should we just defend against them or attempt to heal them? Are we attracting their negativity in order to learn something about ourselves or do we need to learn to be more careful? Or do we need to be sensitive because we know that some day we, too, will play the role of the moth. Life's challenges continue to present themselves wherever we go, so we constantly make judgment calls and learn to protect ourselves in new ways. Traveling in dreams is no different.

When we travel out into the ocean of our magic nights, we are like children. We can't always see danger coming. We might choose to bring protectors and teachers and have rules and maps to follow. It takes time to learn these rules, and sometimes an accidental trip off the beaten path will teach us to really understand how to have fun and be safe as well on our journeys.

Over the years I have learned some useful tools and techniques to get what I want, but I have also learned some very important guidelines to make sure that I get what I need, not what I don't need, as safely as possible for everyone involved. There is power in the ocean of dreams—power that needs to be respected but can also bring wonderful gifts if used properly and with the right intentions.

A few years ago on Halloween I spent the weekend at a camping lodge with a local hiking club. We had a great costume party and everyone took part. Some of the people there knew I had some familiarity with things spiritual, and they asked me if I would lead a Ouija board session with them. I told them that there were certain procedures that I would need to guide them through before we started. When I began to explain the safety procedures the party guests lost interest. It was too complicated. I knew very well that calling random spirits forth with no preparation and no safety boundaries was a bad idea and I knew that they, like children going to play in a darkening forest full of wild animals, had no idea what might be out there. In their minds it wasn't going to be fun if I did all the things I felt that I needed to do to protect them and myself. The Ouija board never came out that night.

Fortunately, setting safety boundaries for a magic night is fast and easy. All that's needed are a few of the right words, the right intentions and an understanding of the process. When going on your Magic Nights journey, just like throwing a party, it's important to set a positive mood and make sure you and everyone is safe and has a good time. I will explain in greater detail the specific words to create safety in the chapter: The Magic Words. It is also nice to remember that our shadows, usually created by our own fears, are never more powerful than the lightness of our being.

THE TOOL CHEST

As your tour guide, my Magic Nights tool chest is pretty hefty, and it needs to be. I have gathered many tools over the years and as new experiences come, new tools are created. Some of the tools are used day and night and some languish at the bottom of the chest, forgotten and dusty. Still I respect them all.

Life seems to move very fast these days. Everything changes quickly and it can be hard to keep up. So our personal tool chests become more important. We need a wide variety of tools to make everything we do more efficient and effective. After all, we don't know when the flood, earthquake, snowstorm, divorce, or job change will take us on an unintended, unexpected journey. Even events happening on the other side of the planet can rock our boats right where we live.

When our lives are so full, time becomes even more important. All of our time—waking or sleeping—becomes something we need to use as wisely as we are able to create some stability in our lives and sail forward as gracefully as possible through these waves of uncertainty.

CAPTAIN'S LOG #1: MY LIFE IS...

As you drift off to sleep tonight, imagine looking out into the soft starlit skies of your own Magic Night. Ponder those great universal questions and dream dreams of what you would like in your life and what your world could be like.

In the morning, begin your Magic Nights logbook by completing the phrase: "My Life Is ..." Write down as many answers as you can think of, until you feel complete. Then think about the following phrases.

- What are your favorite positive phrases about your life?
- What limiting phrases would you prefer not to say, but find yourself saying anyway? What phrases do other people use about themselves that you would like to be true for you as well?
- What phrase would you like to be true for you first?

COMMON LIMITING OR UNLIMITING PHRASES:

Easy for you to say.
You have to work hard.
I'll just have to get used to it.
(i.e. a chronic health condition)
I'm having a senior moment.
It isn't what it used to be.
Set for Life.
Life is hard.
Just Lucky I guess.
More money than God.
Things just have a way of working themselves out.
A natural athlete.
The face of an angel.
Good genes.
I don't know how they do it.
I wish I could do that.

ABOUT YOUR TRAVEL GUIDE

I have traveled the oceans of the unseen both during the day and at night since I was small. A few near-death experiences as a child taught me that there was real help and support out there beyond my world. At that time, leaving my body was a matter of survival. However, it allowed me to see and experience what was possible and to know that for the most part this intangible realm, wherever it might be, was fundamentally a place of unconditional love and support. In fact, because of the circumstances of my waking physical life, I decided at that time that real people were either neutral or dangerous and that the only help and solace that I could count on was out there with my angels, helpers and guides. Thankfully, in the years since then I have had an enormous amount of healing and support from both realms and this connection deepens daily. More importantly, I have learned to enjoy the adventure of being here on this earth and to welcome sharing the joy and friendship I find here.

Perhaps because of this beginning, my personal goals seem to be more internal than external. I have a habit of setting my sights on the highest intellectual, conceptual, spiritual mountain I can find and then putting one foot in front of the other until I reach the top. If someone like Deepak Chopra challenges me in a quantum physics fashion to go beyond the points of attention and understand the waves of the field of all possibilities, I will get on my surfboard and go out there looking for the biggest wave of energy I can find.

I like the possibility of all possibility. I like the idea that those atoms in the universe can rearrange themselves in all that empty space just on our say-so, and that waves of beautiful music can come of that. If someone like Sondra Ray says physical immortality is possible, I say, "How do I get there?" If I hear someone say I want to be a millionaire, I say, "Teach Me how it feels to be a billionaire."

Sometimes ambition can seem like a recipe for disappointment, but I believe that the journey forward to any of these goals, if cared for in the moment, is equally as powerful and beautiful as the goal itself. So where do you want to go? What do you want to do? The universe is a great ocean of unlimited love, abundance, power and potential, and it is waiting for you. Just say the magic words …

PRAYERS OF OUR ANCESTORS

SETTING AN INTENTION

Words create emotions. Emotions create a physiological change in the body. You may tense up when you're angry, or hold your breath when you're afraid. You probably have some of your own favorite sayings or quotes that get you motivated, get you out of a funk or just get you laughing. I'm sure that you can think of a few memories, stories or books that have inspired you as well. As humans, we invent our own stories to help us understand our lives. We may personify things so that we can communicate with them more easily. We talk to pictures and pets, and we even talk to "God" as if God were a white bearded old man when God is also widely described as being an asexual creative force which exists everywhere and in everything.

Because of the ways in which we connect with everything around us, our dreams can also be a source of information for us. The power of our human brain to invent scenarios that become our own personal stories to teach or warn us is something that scientists are just beginning to understand. Right there in our heads, most of our brain lies dormant most of the time and it's probably chock full of untold talents and magical powers. It's just patiently waiting for us to take the helm and give it our instructions.

You can be religious, spiritual, or live scientifically in the here and now. Luckily, this type of intention setting doesn't judge or care. Everyone can be happy and fulfilled. Everyone can choose to be a loving and ethical person. Some of us, because of where we were born and raised, led lives predetermined to be immersed in a particular spiritual path. Bathed in its structure, we find peace. For others it is more a matter of familial and personal choice perhaps taking us on a purely scientific path. There may also be a variety of spiritual paths which blend in our lives, creating the comfort we crave in a world of change, mystery and uncertainty.

No matter how you access the abundant resources and mysteries of the universe, these resources, like the trillions of atoms they are made of, move through nearly empty space. They are infinite, flexible, and can be very powerful—and they are available to everyone. No matter what the story, no matter what the setup or scenario you are comfortable with, just know that your brain, in concert with that part of the universe that is an unlimited unknowable resource, can work for you all night long. It can do as you ask if you take the time to tell it what you want.

CAPTAIN'S LOG #2: PONDERING YOUR BRAIN

- How big is the part our brains play in creating our personal universes?
- Do our brains create stories and characters just to help us make sense of things like the rhythms, patterns and forces that affect our survival?
- How much do we personify things and forces so that we can relate to them and 'communicate' to them?
- Does this help us?
- How would you define someone who is called psychic? Intuitive? Sensitive?
- Do you think you can be psychic?
- Are we all psychic in different ways?
- Would you like to expand your awareness of the universe around you?
- How would you like that to look?
- What do you think your brain could be capable of if you used it in its full capacity?
- Can you imagine that there is a superconscious part of you that has a bigger view and understanding of the universe?
- Would you call this your high self or your inner wisdom or your authentic self or your guardian angel?
- What would it feel like to have this kind of big picture about your life?

The first step in the Magic Nights process is to set your intention. You will use certain words to set the stage, the words that tell your mind, your body, and whomever or whatever happens to be listening, what you want and need. From the dawn of time, humanity has felt the need to cry out to the universe, to cry out to something bigger than themselves for help. The word we usually attach to this cry for help is "prayer."

PRAYER AND RELIGION

Most people think of prayer and immediately think of religion, but prayer can be called any number of things - meditation, contemplation, intention, or spell casting, all depending on which cup of rules and definitions of the great unknown you happen to be drinking from. These cups are an important part of our sustenance as human beings. We seek out the one that rejuvenates and nourishes us in such a way that we feel our cup will "runneth over."

Though I have repeatedly attempted to settle down and fit in to my world, this type of life doesn't appear to be my destiny. I have never been one to drink from a single cup for very long. I tell my friends that if someone were to try to put me in a box, categorize me or jail me through some external, immutable definition of me, that my elbows would come out very quickly. One of my favorite responses is "I do unless I don't. I will unless I won't. I reserve the right to change my mind in any moment." In practice, I tend to spend some time within a particular spiritual path that I'm drawn to at the moment and wander about for a while. I have fun making friends and collecting tools for my tool chest. But often find myself leaving sooner than I expected. Then I pause, take a breath and look for a new spiritual adventure.

DIVINE PAPER CUPS

Years ago, a friend sent a couple of young men to my house to talk to me about their faith. I didn't know much about their particular religious organization, but I wanted to honor my friend's loving intentions. Also, I am never one to turn down the opportunity for spirited theological debate. I accepted.

At one point, they pulled out about a dozen small paper cups. They stacked them up into a delicate pyramid shape, saying that Jesus was at the top. This was an analogy to their church structure, in that if you do certain things and climb the steps of the pyramid in the proper order and with the proper training, you might move further up the pyramid. They were happy within their structure. It suited them at that point in their lives and was the place from which they were learning what their souls needed to learn. Since they came to me, I was going to answer their call with my own version of the cups of theology.

I asked the boys if they needed to keep their cups, as I was going to get creative. They didn't. As they continued to talk, I disassembled their pyramid. I then found a pin and poked some holes in one side of each cup. One group of holes was in the shape of a cross, another a crescent moon, another a Native American prayer wheel. On the other side of one of the cups I ripped the edge a little and folded it back, like a door. I put the cups, open side down, in a loose circle, and put the holes so that they faced the center of the circle. In the center, I put a small candle. Then I described what I had done.

Pointing to the cups I said, "These represent religions, large and small: Christianity, Islam, Hinduism, Buddhism, Native American Spirituality. The holes represent the way each religion sees God, Goddess—or both—or the Great Spirit. There is light and truth in all of them, and outside of them as well." I then pointed to the candle in the middle, indicating "God."

I continued, pointing to the ripped door in the demonstration model. "The door to the church is here," seemingly away from the light. So we come into the church from the outside world, the space surrounding the cups, so that we can see the light. The light is in the shape and colors that we like, or that we are just used to. And the light gives us a cosmic Vitamin D that we as humans all need.

Atheists, or just those who are really busy in their waking lives, aren't attracted to what's in the cups, but it doesn't mean they live in some other universe. They live in the same one as the rest of us, and the light is there for them as well, perhaps in a beautiful setting in nature, or in a wonderful new scientific discovery, or in the eyes of a loving pet. It doesn't need a name or a definition to feel warm and good, so they get as much as they want as well.

I was born into one of these cups. I know all the usual hymns. My mother was an ordained minister of the United Methodist church. But as I have wandered a bit in this life, I've spent time in a number of different cups. I've sweated in a sweat lodge. I sang chants in Hindu and Sanskrit. I've taken communion and played volleyball with the Episcopals and toned heavenly Oms with my New Age friends. There are wonderful tools and sources of inspiration in all of these paths.

With the boys, I didn't feel that it was necessary to tell them all these details. I just finished my demonstration by saying, "My goal is to be here." I pointed to a space in between the cups and the candle. They paused a moment, then continued with their scripts. I listened to them, and I believe that they had listened to me too.

CAPTAIN'S LOG #3: PONDERING THE UNIVERSE

- Do you think the universe is fundamentally neutral, good or dangerous?
- Is it possible that there are parallel universes or multiple universes?
- Are there dimensions to the universe that we can't perceive as humans?
- Do you believe in extra-terrestrial beings, angels or other sentient beings that exist in our universe?
- Are they among us now?
- Are they trying to help us or competing with us?
- How much love is there to go around in the universe?
- What if love were just energy flowing abundantly in ease and harmony?
- Can spirituality help people understand the unknown?
- Is that good?
- Are spirituality and superstition just ways to explained things to us that science will one day explain better?
- Have you had spiritual or other experiences that you can't explain, but that feel very real to you?
- How did they feel?
- What did they make you feel about your universe?

WANDERING AND GATHERING TOOLS

Not only have I wandered spiritually, but Spirit has seen to it that I wander physically as well. Some friends have even suggested that I just get a house on wheels. My childhood years were spent moving as a result of the old corporate habit of moving people to keep them loyal. My father worked as a salesman for a large lumber company and, like clockwork, every three years or so we would pack up and move to some other town in some other state.

Finally, he started his own company and we settled in suburban Maryland. I stayed in the Washington, D.C. area into my twenties. I married and then divorced. Then I began my journey into more serious meditation and healing. I decided I wanted to be a doctor, so I moved to the Midwest to go to Chiropractic school. I graduated, but opportunities didn't come there. Soon the Rocky Mountains called to me. I thought I might just breathe that fresh air forever. But a mere four years later, my newly finished screenplay in hand, I was on a train to Los Angeles. But that city also had it's day. And when it's day was over I drove back across the country and came "home" to my family in New Jersey.

Still my car seems to idle impatiently. I am getting older, and hopefully wiser, but there are still many places I'd like to go. As a result, this carpetbag full of tools is becoming more and more critical. I want it to be chock full of things that make my travels more efficient. I have no more time to gradually, gently handle the obstacles, the fear sets, and the old inefficient subconscious mental programming that seems to be holding me back.

CAPTAIN'S LOG #4: THE POWER TO CHOOSE

- Do you like to fit in or be a trailblazer or a little of both?
- What are your biggest fears? How much do your fears control your life?
- How much power do you feel you have in your life?
- How are you creative?
- What are you passionate about?
- What do you want in life?
- What do you choose to have in your life?
- What good things would you feel comfortable accepting into your life?
- What do you think about the idea that the universe merely gives you what you expect, as if it is replying with a resounding "YES" to every assumption and statement you make about your life?
- What would you like to say to the universe right now about your life,
- knowing that it will wholeheartedly agree?

PRODUCTIVE SLEEP

Choosing the big goals means working smart. So wouldn't it be nice to be able to keep moving toward them during my sleep as well as my waking hours? How could all those hours asleep be programmed to keep me moving forward? I heard about sleep hypnosis tapes and tried a few, but found them useful only to a certain point. The feelings and goals in those programs weren't tailored closely enough to my specific needs and desires. I wanted to design my own program, in my own words and in my own style. You could call it a prayer, but I saw it as a setting of intention— talking firmly to myself and invoking that inner wisdom. Then for good measure and safety, inviting all those in other dimensions who might choose to help me.

BEDTIME PRAYERS, HISTORICALLY

For many, a bedtime prayer brings to mind that simple verse of childhood: "Now I lay me down to sleep, I pray the Lord my soul to keep, And should I die before I wake, I pray the Lord my soul to take." As we grow older, these simple words can fall by the wayside. But they are replaced with the wise advice to "just sleep on it" if you are trying to find a solution, a new idea or approach to a problem.

As I grew, I also understood that prayers generally happened in church and I had learned not to expect any direct answer or response. Ask for world peace, ask for compassion for others, ask for mercy for all evil deeds or thoughts, and ask quietly. If prayers were more colorful and dramatic with the use of images, smells, or motion to enhance the experience, then they might be called a spell and by the definition of many, evil.

On the other hand, meditation is also a kind of prayer—a quietness, an awareness cultivated in private, with few rules or complications. If you meditated long enough and were able to quiet your mind for long enough, some kind of revelation might happen. Some kind of peace might be achieved. It seemed to me that one half of the world prays by asking and the other half prays by listening.

Then I found myself at a Native American sweat lodge with a peace pipe in my hand. As I was instructed in the use of the pipe, I discovered that in this type of prayer both asking and listening are included harmoniously. As with the Christian or Jewish faiths, the Native Americans invite the spirit of the divine, be it in human or animal form. They invite the knowingness and the wisdom of those beings who have a larger perspective. There is a time for speaking, and then there is a time for listening. It is a very balanced and grounded spirituality. Because the Native Americans have lived closely with the land for so long, their practices resonate with the earth and trees and rocks in a way that has always been very soothing for me.

A NATIVE AMERICAN SWEAT LODGE

South of St. Louis there was a camp with cabins, a small lake and a central shared dining hall. It was here that a Yaqui Indian had built and consecrated a lodge and had been leading sweats for some time. It was there, on a cold New Years day, that I experienced my first Native American sweat lodge.

I know now that not all sweat lodges are the same. Some are dangerous, and some are designed to be a more gentle cultural education. Lucky again, I was introduced to the sweat lodge and spiritual tradition surrounding it by someone of integrity who was sensitive enough, or if you like, psychic enough, to monitor and steer the emotional energy in the lodge so that it was safe and productive. This sweat lodge was a physical challenge and not for the faint of heart. The heat and steam would push us to the limits of our endurance, putting our bodies under stress to the point where some physiological survival mechanisms were activated.

Though the environment was carefully controlled, all of the normal defenses and emotional resistance fell away without any chemical interference from drugs or mind-altering substances. There were a few additives, the first being "All Our Relations," which referred to all life and spirit. These relations included spirit helpers as well as tree and rock people, animal clans and brothers and sisters of human clans. They were invited and invoked by the phrase (phonetic approximation here) "Ah Ho, Matahqui Wayahsin." Also drumming, song, sharing, natural tobacco in a peace pipe and the drifting aromatic smoke of smudge sticks made of sage, sweetgrass and cedar created this natural sacred space.

Once in the lodge, the fire tender put red-hot rocks from the mother fire into a depression in the middle of the lodge. Then the canvas flaps were pulled down to the ground and we were in complete darkness. Our sweat leader then used a gourd to scoop water from a bucket and throw it onto the fire. The steam began to rise. We could hear it and feel it, but it was pitch black and very cramped in the lodge. We huddled together and waited as it steadily got hotter. The leader put some pleasant smelling herbs or cedar on the rocks and then he started leading a sharing and praying process.

The ceremony was a purification. In an effort to find relief from the growing heat, I put my face in the mud on the floor and kept myself covered with my towel. More water was thrown on the hot rocks and as another blast of steam rose. The leader instructed us to sing louder and pray harder. We obeyed and somehow it worked. Somehow it brought relief from the heat. I did my best fake Lakota at the top of my lungs, and just when I thought I couldn't stand it anymore a scoop of water was thrown in my face. Moments later the flaps came up on the sides of the lodge and I could see the woods outside and breathe fresh air. I felt cleansed and pure in a natural, smoky, muddy kind of way. After four of these "doors" we waded into the pond next to the lodge to cool off. Then the brave or more experienced sweat-ers would go in for another four doors. At the end of the sweat, my hair would smell like that fragrant smoke and sage. I always liked that smell.

After I had attended a number of sweats at this lodge, and earned respect by regularly going in for all eight doors, the leader honored me by crafting a peace pipe as a gift for me. He carved the stem and soft stone in the shape of an eagle's head and gave me instructions on how to use it in my own private ceremonies. It was at this point that I learned the full Native American version of prayer. I was instructed to do a seven-day prayer cycle to consecrate the pipe. This is how it went:

THE PEACE PIPE CEREMONY

A health warning: This ceremony contains tobacco, which is highly addictive and unhealthy for people if used on a regular basis, especially those with any heart and/or lung conditions. This ceremony is an illustration of process. Most of it is not part of the regular Magic Nights sleep-programming routine.

CREATING SACRED SPACE:

First I find a place outdoors where my view is, as much as possible, of pure nature. It should be away from electronics of any kind and not present a fire hazard. I carefully unwrap my pipe from its red blanket cover. Inside the wrap I have matches, incense, a smudge stick, some crystals, organic pipe tobacco, and the pipe, its stem wrapped in one piece of cotton cloth and the bowl in another.

I set up the incense and light it, checking the wind direction and placing it so that the smoke wafts over me gently. I light the smudge stick and smudge, or purify myself, as well as the immediate area, with the fragrant smoke. I set the smudge stick, still smoking, in a shell or fireproof container in front of me. Then I unwrap the stem and bowl.

25

At this point, the ceremony may not be strictly by the book. Still it has a wonderful effect. I think the intention of setting sacred space, or building a 'church' in nature and dressing the altar is the most important ingredient. Though the details, the scenery and the props may change (I have had powerful written ceremonies at my desk, without the pipe or props, right in front of my computer), setting the intention for a positive and enlightening experience is the foundation for the ceremony.

INVITING:

Once that the stage is set, I invite the helping spirits, power animals, and any other beings of love and light that might want to share in the ceremony. The key word here, which I will reiterate and stress through this book, is *"invite."* You certainly don't want anyone or anything there that doesn't want to be there.

After putting the bowl securely on the stem, I give each pinch of tobacco an intention and purify it in the smudge smoke before putting it in the pipe bowl. Then I lift the pipe to the sky and invite the four directions, turning the pipe clockwise in a circle each time.

GRATITUDE AND COMPASSION:

At this point, now that the helpers, healers, and guides are all in attendance, my heart space needs to be opened. It is time to do gratitudes and pray for others.

I say thank you to everything and everyone that has been helpful or inspiring, in my life. Typically about ten gratitudes will feel right. Then I pray with compassion and love for two other people. I do not ask that they receive what I, in my mind, think they need; I ask for pure uncategorized unconditional love and compassion and blessings that their souls can use as they choose. Puff, puff, puff ...

26

It must be said that tobacco can be gently mind-altering along with being highly addictive. It gently opens the mind and senses in a way that is calming and useful for this type of ceremony. Though I will not inhale for much of the ceremony (as a precaution for myself, I only inhale when doing a one-time only ceremony), the effect will be carried in the smoke around me.

SPEAKING FROM THE HEART:

Next, I open my heart and tell the universe about my pain and fear. I unload to my heart's content. I whine and I complain. But since anger is just a reaction to fear or another way of crying out for love, I know it's not appropriate here. Neither is blame, since blame says "I don't really want to change anyway," and fixes nothing. I know I am heard by compassionate beings, so I attempt to be polite, but also trust in the sacred space I have created. I speak with honesty and self-compassion until I feel empty and no more words come.

ASKING:

Now, politely, I get to ask for something specific with the understanding that it be *"according to free will and for the highest good of all"* and *"with love and light."* Puff, puff, puff...

LISTENING:

I quiet my mind again. It's easier to listen intently now since I have done all the preparation. If I am not actually out in nature, or can't see it, I go inside my mind and visualize myself there, waiting for someone to come up to me with some really great advice and maybe a gift of healing or great energy. Of course, stray thoughts do come through. I just quickly shut them off and return to listening for that quiet soothing voice—that voice and presence that just feels right, true, and good. Sometimes, right at first I hear a loud voice trying to give me advice. I've found that the voice that's too loud and too quick is most often a fearful part of my subconscious trying to steer me away from the real truth and the real message. Practice and discernment over the years have made it easier for me to tell the difference.

For instance, I have found that my inner voice is good at some things and not so good at others. When I am awakened by a voice that says "Get Up!", and it's earlier than I planned on getting up, I've found there is usually a reason. Perhaps there's an accident on the freeway and it will take longer to get where I am going, or I don't have any clean clothes. However, my inner voice is notoriously bad at giving me driving directions.

CLOSING THE CEREMONY:

If I have received an answer, be it in words, pictures, concepts or feelings, and when I feel complete, it is time to finish and open the ceremonial circle. If I feel complete even in the absence of an answer, it's also time to finish and open the circle. Words of gratitude are important now. I address them to all helpers present, seen or unseen. It's as if the ceremony is like a party. These guests came, and I really liked having them there. I would like them to want to come to my next party as well, so I need to make sure they feel welcome.

One phrase that I have used, drawn from other kinds of ceremonial gatherings, is: *"The circle is open but unbroken. Merry meet, merry part, and merry meet again. Blessed be."* Then I carefully clean the site and pack my pipe away.

ITINERARY #1: FIRST JOURNEYS

You are ready to push your boat further from shore, to go on your first journeys to experience the power of your mind and the magic of the ocean of the universe. Use the words below to set out on your first journeys. For the best results, I recommend to choose one goal and intention and go on the same journey for at least four nights in a row.

At night, spend five minutes setting your intention in three steps: Ship Shape, Put On your Captain's Uniform and Set Your Destination.

SHIP SHAPE:

Check the weather and make sure your boat is sound and safe.
In love and light, love and light, love and light (and joy / harmony / peace / etc.)
According to free will and for the good of all (and for my highest and best good)

PUT ON YOUR CAPTAIN'S UNIFORM:

I call forth my authentic self, my higher mind, my inner wisdom and my divine heart to be with me during my sleep and dreaming time tonight.

SET YOUR DESTINATION:

It is best to be general during your first journeys. Use the words in the examples below. Reading the text of Magic Nights will help you understand why I find these phrases work best.

Please teach me how to feel completely rested, refreshed and ready for the new day when I awaken in the morning at the perfect time.

Or

*Please teach me how to feel completely whole, healthy and well
in my body (strong / graceful / beautiful / handsome / resilient)*

Or

*Please teach me how to feel financially healthy, well and wise,
for my highest and best good.*

IN THE MORNING, LISTENING AND FINDING YOUR TREASURES:
This is where you will begin to have a direct experience
of the treasures you have brought back with you from your Magic
Nights Journey. Thank your inner guidance and wisdom and
whomever may have helped you during the night. Then open your
treasure chest and see what's inside!
When you awaken, hit the snooze button on your alarm. Tune
inside to your mind and body - how do you feel? What do you
remember about what you asked for? Did you dream? How did
you feel in your dreams (no matter how random they may be).

DURING THE DAY:
Pay attention to what happens and how you feel about life.
Pay attention to how people respond to you. What does this tell
you? What surprising opportunities come your way?

CAPTAIN'S TRAVELOGUE AND TOOL CHEST

MEDITATION

I wasn't always this way. I used to think I wanted all the normal things in life—a husband, family, some kind of appropriate career—but a whole new world opened up to me at the age of thirty. At the time I was studying holistic bodywork and I had some new friends who had a metaphysical, New Age lifestyle. Perhaps a few near-death experiences as a child had something to do with it as well. Nevertheless, some confluence of events, stars, and destiny thrust me into previously uncharted inner waters and those inner waters were full of waves, storms, strange lands, wild creatures and beautiful ones. There wasn't much in my quiet Protestant upbringing that had prepared me for this or had given me any tools to handle it.

TALKING BACK

At first, it was like a door had opened in my head. Though what was coming in didn't make me a full psychic—I didn't see the future or ghosts or auras—it was enough to make my mind very busy. This door opened to allow people, living or dead, to come into my mind. I first experienced it when I thought about someone, or thought of what I'd like to say to them. It was as if they were in the room hearing everything I had said, hearing all my thoughts about them—and then they would talk back! Judging by the responses I got, the part of the person that talked back was typically a reactive, annoying and uncontrolled part of them which they were probably unaware of on any conscious level. My mind was no longer a private universe and playground where I could be either happy or whiney or angry whenever I wanted. Suddenly, there were consequences.

First I argued with them or tried to tell them to shut up or go away. I was completely unsuccessful. So I began to try to control my thoughts. No anger or reactive thought was allowed because it would just become a brawl in my head. I knew that learning to control my thoughts wasn't going to be easy, but It was all I could do at the moment. And that wasn't the only new development in my suddenly sort-of-psychic universe.

REALLY BIG LESSONS

In addition to the insane asylum that was holding meetings in my head, I was also thrown into long and sometimes terrifyingly deep and powerful meditations at all times of day. Some large being or entity, Zeus for example, would come and take me somewhere to teach me some really big lesson on the workings of the universe. I learned things like balancing a dark flame and light flame in each hand, which resulted in somehow growing large and powerful, and how Compassion plus Balance equals Love, all in a perfect triangle. And, not least, I was told to pretend I was God or Goddess and proceed through the creation of the world in the usual seven-day format. Talk about performance anxiety. Not that I wasn't grateful for all the help and lessons coming from wherever these beings came from. For the most part, they seemed benevolent and wise, but these meditations could go on for hours, and appropriate timing didn't seem to matter to them.

I remember one such occasion, when I was nearly through with the "Create the world in seven days" lesson. They, whomever they were, wanted me to do this very important task when I just happened to be stuck in traffic on the Washington, D.C. Beltway. I was just driving along, mildly bored and annoyed. Then I got a creepy-crawly feeling down the back of my neck. At that point the teacher of the day made himself apparent to me and began to give instructions. It's really hard to say no to some really magnificent being when they are so lovingly generous with their deep and significant universal wisdom. I remember that I positioned my car behind a big tractor-trailer and hooked up a mental tractor-beam to its rear brake lights. It wasn't enough. I was just too distracted and I pulled off the freeway.

I decided that, despite my gratitude for the wisdom and teachings, this arrangement couldn't continue as it was. It was simply hazardous, both outwardly and inwardly. I had to get better control of my mind. And after having to play God/Goddess and create the world as best I could, I became rather concerned that what was going on in my head was actually having some kind of effect on something or someone out in the world or in the universe. If I was really doing all this really important stuff that my guides wanted me to do, I certainly didn't want to create any messes for anyone, including myself.

I have to admit I felt challenged. The inner Capricorn goat in me saw a really big mountain and wanted to climb it to see what was on the other side. So, goat-like, I began to methodically put one foot in front of the other.

WHERE'S THE RULE BOOK?

First I went looking for answers, structure and some kind of rule book. I am generally a "tools and rules" kind of person. It makes me feel safer in the world. So whatever worlds I would be traveling in, I wanted to feel that I had some guidelines. Although I knew I could probably just turn the voices and visions off if I tried hard enough, I didn't want to do that. I couldn't do it. It would feel like pouring concrete over a field of wildflowers—wildflowers that happened to produce the Elixir of Life. There were whole new universes to explore, but I wanted to make sure to do it right. I didn't want to hurt anyone, but I did want to take home any new tools and techniques I might find that could be fun and useful. Luckily for me—and I've usually been very lucky this way— the perfect helpers, in the form of real flesh and bones people, began to walk into my life.

Though it would seem to be a natural progression, none of these helpers were Christian or Jewish mystics. I simply didn't have access to them at the time. I know now that because of all the historical assumptions and dogmas built up around those religions their traditions wouldn't have given me the freedom to explore the way I did. I needed someone who was okay with Zeus, or others like him, being in my group of non-physical teachers. No loving, helpful, wise and divinely inspired being was going to be turned away, no matter where they came from or what religious practices may have been built up around them.

I could already hear the backlash in my head. Anyone except the approved list of wise persons is evil. There would be dead silence if I mentioned that I was in church thinking about Jesus and he showed up in my mind and we had an amiable conversation. Prayer only goes so far in many religious traditions. Devotees don't expect a direct answer, and probably wouldn't trust it if they got one. Only mystics and saints seemed to be exempt and I certainly didn't have the qualifications for those titles.

Even so, I still wanted—and needed—some rules. I wanted good rules from a good, loving and safe place. I wanted rules that made sense to me, and made sense for the time and place I was in. If the universe was sending me all kinds of wisdom, love and healing, I surely didn't want to limit the way it was presented to me. I didn't want someone who had never traveled in those astral realms between conscious life and death to bind me with human-invented judgments or dogmas. I didn't want their fears to turn me away from the love that was obviously being offered to me in huge quantities and in many colorful, yet challenging, forms.

The Eastern spiritual traditions didn't seem to have answers for me at this stage either. While they do practice meditation, it is a path deeper into silence and peaceful presence. This is a valuable tool to have, but there was nothing quiet or silent about where my mind was going—in fact quite the opposite. The other realms were aggressively seeking me out and taking me on wild adventures.

That left two reasonable options: the Pagan or Wiccan system, which is very colorful and creative about working in other states of mind and other realms, and the Native American "journeying" system of meditation, which is very grounded and natural, with its deep and long shamanic tradition of astral travel and power animals. Soon I ended up exploring both, but opportunity dictated that my first footfall in my astral travel education was into the realms of the Pagans.

In those days, before gaming and virtual worlds, the dungeons and dragons, Renaissance Fairs, and Magical Mystery Tour crowds would gather just as they do now; to share the same magic and mystery, the same connection and honoring of the divine in all forms as they have for eons. I liked the fancy dress and the drumming circles and, lets face it, I was pretty good at things of a mystical bent. Being observant, I was naturally curious as to what the pentagrams around their neck really meant. When I asked, one simply replied, "There are good Christians and bad Christians, good Wiccans and bad Wiccans." Then I discovered how ancient and archetypal the symbol was, and that many spiritual traditions used it. Symbolism was important in this community. And their world seemed as safe as any. It was just more colorful than most that I had experienced. I also had the benefit of an inner intellectual sort of self-righteousness. This, coupled with using common sense and trusting my instincts has been a lifelong form of self-defense for me in a frequently non-sensical world. This has always been far more powerful than my fear of the unknown. So, with living, breathing Wiccan friends as inspiration, I stepped into a metaphysical book shop and into their world.

POSITIVE MAGIC

One of the first books I discovered was called *Positive Magic* by Marion Weinstein. It was an excellent primer for me. It unraveled a lot of the hype about "witchcraft", explaining clearly, sensibly, and historically the sources of discomfort that the fearful like to latch onto. It defined white, grey and black magic and described the various systems of Pagan practices. This approach was good for someone like me who, in a childlike bid for personal safety, feels compelled to know the rules, to blend in and not attract too much attention—to be a good person, but not gullible. This book explained clearly the "dos and don'ts" of working with visions, energies and rituals and other things magical and unseen.

One primary rule it stressed was that what you think about really does affect the world around you and the people in it. It's like an expanded version of the Golden Rule: Do unto others as you would have them do unto you. Suddenly I realized that from this moment on, I not only had to monitor what I did, but where my mind was going. I understood that for all of us, the energy generated by our thoughts, which we can control, affects not only the health of our body, but affects our relationships with our world in a very direct and reactive way.

This discipline seemed so much more demanding than any in the Christian religion I grew up with. It seemed to me that all you had to do to be a good Christian was make it appear to others that you were. What happened under the surface didn't seem to count much, at least not until you were dead. Not so in this philosophy from the Wiccans which demanded that everything you send out or create has consequences, including your thoughts.

The consequences work on the "rule of three," meaning that whatever you put out in thought, word, or deed would return to you three times in the same quality. The return could happen quickly or be delayed until the next life, but you would get back what you put out sooner or later. It was a universal rule, a cosmic balancing act; like a drop of water falling into a pond. The ripple effect would spread and eventually the motion set in place by that drop would return in large sweeping waves over the same place where the drop fell.

All of a sudden, I could feel the cosmic eye on me, those karmic wheels turning one way or the other in response to everything I thought or did. Was I having vengeful thoughts about someone? Was I just yammering on inside my head in a gossipy and catty way? According to this rule, by doing so, somewhere on some universal phone line, the person whom I was thinking about was actually being affected by my thoughts. And I would remember that the next time I saw them. Haven't we all been angry with someone, and then, later, when we looked him or her in the face trying to be neutral, we felt a little guilty and awkward?

I only spent a few years with the Pagan crowd, but things I learned then have stayed with me and have an honored place in my tool chest and rulebook. One of the phrases I use the most, before every meditation and to qualify every request is *"according to free will and for the highest good of all.*" It seemed like common sense to me that everything in life should follow this rule. Everything, without exception. Apparently not only am I a "karma-phobe," but I also don't ever want to be accused of being manipulative just for the satisfaction of my own ego. How am I to know what the universe, in any moment, has planned for someone? How am I to know with any certainty what is actually best for them?

LIKE A THERAPIST

Another bit of good fortune at this time in my life was that I was training at advanced levels to be a holistic body worker and therapist. As a result, when confronted with those subconscious untidy parts of myself and others, I just put on my therapist hat and gently corralled the insanity rather than just going insane myself. I was taught a way of connecting with myself and others in a very intuitive, accepting and honoring way. It is certainly not the only way to heal. Medical science has its own way of working miracles, but, in the case where physical, energetic, and emotional factors all come into play at once, this method can be very effective in addition to other appropriate care.

One of the rules that I was given, which I come back to again and again, is that when working this way, the therapist has to put his or her mind aside and "blend" with the client, listening intently to the signals and directions that are given by the client's body. Rather than using the mind to diagnose, then treat, as science does, this method treats, then diagnoses. The rule for this kind of intuitive energetic healing is that if you decide in your rational mind, based on your conscious experience and expertise, what is wrong with someone and come up with a diagnosis and treatment plan based on that diagnosis, there are too many factors that are not considered. The body is so complex that in order to get to the actual root cause of a dysfunction, a therapist must listen to the body's "inner physician" and follow its lead. If the thinking mind gets in the way, this kind of holistic treatment will be ineffective most of the time.

As a therapist using this type of technique, I have found these principles to be true. When I follow the energetic signals the body is giving me, the body can come up with the most wonderful and perfect solutions that I know I could never have imagined, and when I have strayed too far into my thinking mind during therapy, I have on occasion been chastised by the client's inner physician for not listening. I am only responsible for following prudent rules of courtesy and well-being in general. I can offer love and caring, but not in a way that is conditional to what I think, in my mind, is good for a person. Therefore, "according to free will and for the good of all" still seems like a pretty good rule of conduct for me, on all levels.

In *Magic Nights*, the science involved is very fuzzy. It is truly an unexplored land where your intuition, wisdom, flexibility, and acceptance, both of yourself and others and of the magic of the universe, is key to getting the most out of your journeys.

INVITE

Another very important word that I remember when doing this kind of night work is *invite*. No matter whom I am inviting and no matter what tradition says, even when inviting Jesus or Mother Mary, I still invite. I never call or invoke, because that would not allow for free will. I invite my highest and best helpers, healers and guides to my meditation, and the phrasing typically goes: *"I invite (so-and-so or the essence of so-and-so) according to free will and for my highest good and the highest good of all."* After all these years, I might say to myself that they all ought to know by now that my intention is always set in this frame, but I say it anyway in case someone out there thinks they are going to slip by me and muck things up in my inner journey. No matter how pure of intention I might imagine myself to be, there will always be those out there who would challenge me and teach me. Though I do not seek them out, I know they will come from time to time when I am ready to be tested and taught again, so I am keep my magic nights tool bag handy.

THE SHAMAN'S WAY

During these first few years of meditating, I found a book called *Way of the Shaman* by Michael Harner. It was my introduction to Native and South American shamanistic techniques. It filled in some gaps in my understanding of what was happening to me, and in the back of the book, I discovered an organization called The Foundation for Shamanic Studies, which Harner had organized. Hallelujah. Rules, groups, and method, all clearly defined, and there was a group that met near where I was living.

One of the things this book explained was how a shaman was chosen in some South American native cultures. The candidate was often someone who, as a child, had more challenges to their life and health than most. The challenges could be in the form of abuse, illness, or simply life-threatening turns of fate. In the minds of these people, this person was already trained, emotionally and energetically, in the abilities one needed to be a successful shaman. Having a near-death or simply very traumatic experience as a child can put the child in the position of having to go "out of body" simply to survive. This out of body experience makes the journey to the other realms as an adult much easier to accomplish because the door has already been opened. Since many of the shamanistic techniques have to do with this kind of journeying for the intention of healing, information, or prophecy, it is necessary to have some sort of inborn or acquired talent. Because healthy, well-adjusted children typically have no need to travel out of their bodies to survive, it typically isn't natural or easy for them.

According to my recollection, I was a prime candidate for being the village shaman. I was ripe for the plucking by beings of other realms, and I apparently had been Officially Plucked. Why, I didn't know. I still am not completely clear on that, but in order to do right, to be "on my purpose", I tell myself that I don't always have to know why I am the way I am, or why I are doing what I are doing. I just have to do my best to accomplish my mission the moment, large or small, and then I have to pay attention in order to see where to put my foot down next.

I went to the back of the book and found out how to contact the Foundation for Shamanic Studies. When I found out the next available meeting night in my area, I went. I entered a quiet, dimly lit yoga studio filled with other spiritual seekers. About fifteen of us went through the paces of drumming and animal dancing to inspire our inner shaman. This was a non-altered event, a rule of the Harner organization. No medicinal help, natural or otherwise, is needed to get into a visionary state. This I already knew: for some of us, along with being dangerous, mind-altering substances only get in the way of our clarity.

The rhythmic drumming was soothing, and intentionally so. It was one of the psychic protections put into place by the ritual. The regular rhythm of the drum will deter the negative energies from interfering with the journeyers, so the drum beat went on through the entire night's travels.

Animal dancing is a wonderful way to connect to earth's energies, and get outside of your daily busy mindset. Pretending to be whatever animal inspires you in the moment (although insects are frowned upon for some reason) and produce the accompanying screeches, growls and hoots that bring authenticity. It was a wonderfully cleansing motion, around the circle, to the deep and steady beat of the drum. Animal dancing is also a way to get out of our adult minds and into our childlike creativity. We rediscover

41

free flowing play movement that we often forget how to do as adults, interacting with other dancers as we pass by them with recognition and glee, finding the strengths of each animal as its energy courses through our bodies.

When we had come to the end of the dancing, we silently lay down on our mats in the circle and were led by the drummer into a world below our own, into the earth to find the inner landscape that would feed us and give us our power through an introduction to our power animal.

It was a wonderfully grounding, healthy and satisfying experience. The rules were very clearly spelled out. The safety net was set and the journey to our inner universe was guided surely by someone who knew. This was certainly a step in the right direction. However, as much as I like to follow rules and be safe, things began to go sideways on the very next journey. First, the journeyer is supposed to have a specific question in mind before they start out on their journey. I had my question all ready, but the beings that were waiting at the door to my journey had other ideas. They said, in effect, "Yeah, that's nice, but we're going to take you somewhere else and show you other things." So much for getting my question answered.

Then I was met by my spirit animal guide and we had a good time getting acquainted, but another animal came in: a spirit animal that was someone else's, not mine. He said that specifically. If someone else's spirit animal had something to say to me, and teach me, I was fine with that. After all, he volunteered.

However, when I shared this with the group after the journey, I was met with scowls from a certain quarter. I had broken the rules already, even if not intentionally. Luckily, my friend whose power animal had volunteered his services was fine with. I just didn't feel guilty. It didn't feel like a bad thing to me. I knew the rules were there for our safety, just as I am firm about my rules of safety in Magic Nights. Yet from time to time in this line of work, things happen that aren't anticipated by those rules. At such points, it becomes a matter of taking what you know, listening to your intuition or gut feelings, and then doing your best in the moment.

It wasn't the last time I broke the group's rules before we parted ways. I went to a weekend workshop on journeying with the Harner people. We were led on a beginner journey. It went fine until I shared my experiences during that day's meditation. I soon found out that I had done what was called a "soul retrieval" and they didn't teach that technique until the advanced workshop. Oh well. By that time, I had gotten what I needed: just enough understanding of the structure, rules and guidelines of this kind of journeying. Many of those rules, good rules, have remained in my tool bag.

THE ROCK LADY

Another earth angel that helped me during this period was someone I will call the Rock Lady. I thought I might be going crazy with the unintended meditations and all the people crowding my thoughts. I needed help. I can't remember how I found her, but I found myself at her home one day, in her sunroom gazing over shelves and shelves of crystals and semiprecious stones in natural and carved shapes.

I was immediately enchanted. She had a wonderful, gentle energy and her rocks looked nice as well. She told me she had energetically tested and cleaned all of them, so they were safe. I was happy about that as I didn't know how to tell a good crystal from a bad one yet. I knew she was going to be my source for crystals for a while.

I perused the glittering selection. With her help, I chose a clear quartz crystal about the size and shape of an egg. She said to keep it in my pocket to keep my energy clear. It was like an energetic air freshener, but I needed to cleanse it energetically every week or so in a running stream of cool water.

While I was there, I thought to mention my problems with the chatter in my head and ill-timed meditations. I was relieved when she said not to worry and that I just needed some time to build my psychic walls back up again—and, by the way, I had the right to set my schedule. No more traffic jam meditations; the times and places I chose would be just fine. The teachers could, and would, wait. She told me that I should drink a lot of water, take a lot of showers, carry the crystal and I would be fine.

Those words were so gently comforting. She seemed to be one of those angels in my life that were sent to help with just the right words and the right tools at the perfect moment. I have a large collection of crystals now. They are still a comforting presence, just as she was.

CAPTAIN'S LOG #5: INNER WISDOM

In the morning, sit down with your coffee or tea, a paper and pen. Clear your mind and tune in to your inner mind. Ask your inner wisdom "What do I need to know right now?" Listen intently for the quiet voice that feels right. Listen for practical advice or a way of looking at things today. Write down what you hear and anything else that comes to mind until you feel complete. Do this every morning to develop a deeper relationship with your inner wisdom and to discover the gifts you have received during your Magic Nights.

THE MAGIC WORDS

A GOOD NIGHT'S SLEEP

When I lived in Los Angeles, I worked for a few years as an "extra" or background actor on film and television productions in the area. Most of the time we were contracted by the day, but film productions sometimes asked for a multi-day commitment. These shoots were usually long and could last from five in the morning until eight at night. Between days we would go home, sleep as well as we could, wake up, and do it all over again. One time I booked myself for a three night shoot. It would be hard to be up all night and sleep during the day, but with all the expected overtime, it would probably pay well, so I reluctantly agreed.

It was a large call. They needed eight hundred extras to report to a small town in the desert outside of Los Angeles every night and migrate purposefully down the main street. I knew that It would be cold outside and it was a 'wet shoot' which meant that in the film, it was supposed to be raining. Luckily, we were allowed to dress warmly and bring umbrellas. We all met at the

47

location base camp at about 5 p.m. to check in. It was a long night of bad coffee, dodging the rain machine and finding some comfort in camaraderie as we were herded about. The sun finally rose. We packed up our things and headed home.

When I finally got myself into my bed and put on my eye mask to block the light coming in the windows, I realized that I would be getting only four hours of sleep. Then I would have to get myself out of bed, get ready and report to the location again. I like my sleep and would prefer to have at least eight hours of it normally. If I was going to make it through all three nights (and get paid all that overtime) without getting sick, I would have to make that four hours of sleep count.

I collapsed onto my pillow and I set my intention with as much firmness as I could muster: I invited in all the help I could think of on all levels, for my highest good. I asked that my sleep be deep and restful, and when I awoke at the perfect time, I would feel completely rested, completely refreshed, and completely ready for the new day. "Thank you, God." I repeated these phrases a few times and directed them to every cell in my body and to every helper out there in the universe, seen or unseen, that would volunteer to help me reach my goals for the night. Then I let myself drift off to sleep.

Three hours fifty-eight minutes later, I woke up just before the alarm went off. I realized I was actually awake and functional! It had worked like a charm. I then tuned inward for a moment to thank all the helpers who had come, and to ask for any advice for the day. After a few minutes, I received my words of wisdom and felt satisfied. I rolled out of bed and began the day happily.

Two nights and two short days later, I was driving home from the last night of shooting. Unlike many of the extras, I had actually made it through all three nights without getting sick or just quitting, even though on the second night, they didn't need the rain machine because it really rained, and rained hard. We were all cold and miserable that whole night.

I realized how well it worked to set my intention before going to bed to get the kind of night's sleep I wanted. From this point forward I began to experiment and set my intention for all kinds of things, one each night. I found myself getting not only what I asked for in the way that was perfect for me, but I realized that many other wonderful surprises were coming my way. I was convinced. I had opened the door to a whole new world of adventure and treasure and I was not going to miss one more night of discovery. In these past eight years I have learned much about that ocean; about what is out there, how to set my course for success, and what to expect. It's been an amazing journey and it's a big, big magical ocean. Are you ready?

SHIP SHAPE: MAGIC WORDS FOR A SAFE AND ENJOYABLE JOURNEY

Get comfortable and sit up straight. Or, if you prefer to lie down, lie flat on your back with your head straight. This will balance the sides of your brain and focus you in the present. First, create a safe space for your nighttime trip by setting the scene and the intention for the best experience possible for you and everyone you invite. You can use some or all of these phrases:

> *In Love and light, By love and light,*
> *According to free will and for the good of all.*
> *For my highest and best good.*
> *In all dimensions, in all aspects, in all time and space.*

You may repeat these words until you feel like every part of you and anyone else that might be interested has heard them clearly. A good thing to remember when setting an intention is that the deeper you resonate the vibration of the words through your body, the more effective the intention will be. Go to that peaceful, joyful place in your mind and resonate every atom of your body with positive emotion when you say the words.

Some manifestation programs say that your state of mind while you are envisioning your desired result will be the state of mind that you are in when you receive it. This means that if you envision getting something, but are resentful or sad when you envision it, then when the thing or condition that you ask for shows up, you will feel that way about receiving it. If you get something you want, you will probably want to feel happy, at ease with receiving it. So think of what you want, according to free will and for the good of all, then throw a big party in your mind. Thank the universe, with its vast resources, for graciously bringing to you your fondest wishes and deepest desires.

DAY TRIPS: GET HAPPY

It's good practice to generate an ecstatically happy state—over nothing at all! Work your face into an easy relaxed smile, then create a happy feeling within. You don't need an image or idea to focus on; in fact, it's better if it can just create the feeling of joy as unattached to any event, image or person. Raise your vibration higher and higher, and spread the happiness to every cell of your body, then think of your life in general and see yourself as the happy place within it. Make sure to keep breathing naturally. Then raise the feeling again to a level that is blissful, then ecstatic. Challenge yourself to hold that state for at least thirty seconds. The longer you can hold it, the more it will become a good habit—no drugs required!

Have you ever seen a picture of something you wanted and every cell in your body said "Yes!, That's It!" That's the feeling you're aiming for. Then make it bigger: add a "Wow!, and at the perfect price!" or "Isn't that incredible that it was there just at the right time, right in my neighborhood!" Now expand this feeling to include your entire life: "Wow, the universe is so great at finding ways to give me what I want. All I have to do is keep my eyes and ears open and keep moving forward one step at a time, and the treasures will be there for me to find! In fact, I wonder what wonderful treasures, miracles and wonderful surprises are waiting out there for me right now?"

The process of setting your night's intention can be sleep-inducing all on its own. So do your best not to fall asleep before you have finished! If you should awaken in the middle of the night and realize you never fully set your intention, you can start it again at that time. If you get all the way to the morning without setting your intention fully, don't worry. If you had already invited some crew or friends to your journey (see below) don't be concerned that they seemingly had nothing to do all night. In my experience, they haven't been disappointed. However, if this happens, it would be a good idea to set aside a little more time for your morning meditation to listen to their advice, as a courtesy. Remember that your crew doesn't need your direction all the time, they just want to help. And it may just be that they agreed with your inner wisdom on that night that sleeping naturally was best for you.

INVITE YOUR CREW

Now you, as the captain, are ready to open your heart and invite your crew. Invite just a few for an elite intimate cruise or be creative and expansive for a grand journey:

SOME CREW AND CRUISE MATES

Why go out every night alone into dreamland? Your Magic Nights ship has plenty of room for crew and friends that you can invite. It's as if your night time is a movie or a virtual world and these are the extras you can invite to travel with you during the night. Invite a couple of friends or invite a whole fleet of ships for a Grand World Service Journey. Your mind can create personifications for all kinds of powers and forces that are for your highest good. Maybe lots of help really is really out there, but you won't know unless you send out invitations. Don't hold back, just remember to be a good host. Courtesy in all realms is a good thing.

There are only two rules when inviting your crew: First, always INVITE them. Do not invoke or call them. However, when you are putting on your captain's uniform you may call forth your own aspects because they are parts of you. Second, don't invite anyone currently or recently living. I find that general, rather than specific invitations are best. And remember to thank your crew in the morning.

Below is a list of examples. If you are unfamiliar with some of these faces, a quick internet search will reveal more about each. Also a visit to a metaphysical bookstore can offer more resources and options from many spiritual traditions, such as the many angels and ascended masters available to you as well as the specific powers and qualities of the animal clans that can help you on your journey.

THE CAPTAIN:

You are the most important crew member. Put on your best captain's uniform and call forth your authentic self, your inner wisdom, your divine nature and your divine oversoul or high self, in perfect wholeness and harmony.

FIRST MATES:

Your guardian angel(s), your favorite (deceased) prophet or spiritual authority figure (remember to invite, not call or invoke)

MASCOTS:

Native Americans call these Power Animals. I recommend inviting the dolphin and whale clans. They are great fun and quite powerful healers and guides, especially on an ocean-going journey. Some other animal clans will bring specific qualities: Birds see clearly, Lions bring courage and strength, Bears bring power and comfort, for example.

GENERAL CREW:

You can invite groups of crew: If you are feeling particularly respectful, you can invite someone's divine nature or loving essence to be present with you for the night; or I recommend inviting all the best guides helpers and healers in the universe for you at the moment (you don't have to specify); or go big with the Archangelic League of the Light and the Ascended Masters.

SPECIALISTS:

Doctors, therapists, advisors, engineers, scientists, alchemists, teachers, etcetera are all happy to come: for instance, Dr. Lorphan of Sirius is a master healer. The Arcturian Council of Light, are also healers. Invite specialized saints, angels and ascended masters. Or let the universe decide by inviting the best and most powerful and most perfect specialist, teacher or advisor for you right now, like a "dentist" if you have dental worries or "financial advisor" if you want guidance with money.

FUN GUESTS:

Lord Maitreya, Master Hilarion, Master Saint Germain, Lord Sananda, Lord Serapis Bey, Master El Morya, Lord Lanto, Master Kuthumi, Paul the Venetian, Mary Magdalene, Mother Mary, Goddess Jezebel, Goddess Alchemeya, Lady Guinevere, Lord Merlin, and Goddess Venus, Lord Solarys and many more ascended masters and teachers in higher vibrational dimensions.

There are some persons I don't recommend inviting. For instance, I have experimented with inviting living persons to my night's journey, and in the most courteous way I could imagine. I have also offered myself as one to invite, but the results were not optimal in either case. For instance, when someone asked me, personally, to come to them in spirit to help them, I knew it when it was happening. I felt the pull of the energy, and I was not completely prepared or in the best mood to help. Then there was the question of payment, or in this case, energy exchange. Once when I had invited the essence of one of my most honored living teachers currently living in this world to come assist me, he did volunteer to come. However, the payment was that I was to be available for his work as well as an energetic payment of services in kind. Fair enough. Very soon after that, I worked for him in his clinic while in meditation until I felt I was back in balance with him.

If you have recently deceased loved ones or friends that you would like to reconnect with, it is best to allow a few years to pass after their transition before inviting their divine presence or essence to visit you. My understanding through other sources and the passing of my own mother, is that the transition period for the deceased is a delicate time. The recently dead generally need time to adjust to their new environment before being available for anyone currently living who has personal needs. If they come to you, then offer your love and simply receive their message or let them know you are okay, even if you might not feel that way. If they seem to need help, invite their guardian angels to come to them and take over transition duties.

Since there so many others who are willing and eager to join you on your night's journey, it shouldn't be hard to leave a few off the invitation list. I have been taught and shown for years that it's perfectly alright to have lots and lots of help during these challenging and fast-moving times. I was specifically given a vision of this so that I fully understood:

I saw myself in space, in my sacred circle in my mind. In front of me was someone I didn't know who was offering to help, and in the background, as far as the eye could see, was a line of beings of all shapes and sizes that were very eager to help me with whatever I wanted. It seemed to stretch out to infinity. And they all seemed eager to help, like people in line to get into an exclusive party. After that, I wasn't shy about asking for help for my night adventures. It was such a comforting experience to understand how much help is really out there for all of us. So this is why I highly recommend that this be among your first requests for your Magic Nights.

CHOOSING A MORE PEACEFUL JOURNEY

What if you are not in the mood to throw a party or have a big adventure? Perhaps life is too confusing and stressful or you are just exhausted. Magical miracles and wonderful surprises feel like they must be on some other planet and you don't even feel like putting one oar in the water, or you don't feel it's safe to try yet. You can't even decide what to ask for and you just want to zone out. Thankfully, the universe within and the universe without both know how to support you no matter how you feel in the moment. You can still make your sleep work for you and move yourself forward. A smaller ship and a tour that is quietly supportive may be more appropriate. You can ask for a spa-like tour, or go on the *"Surrender"* tour. Since releasing your worries and problems can be like a cosmic vitamin, I have included it in the chapter about the Port of Supply. It can also open the door to a deeper understanding of the help that is waiting for you out there in the universe.

FEELINGS AS DESTINATIONS

The magic words in this book are gathered from years of experimentation and have shown themselves to be the ones that produce the fastest and most beneficial results. One phrase that seems to produce an almost immediate effect is:

Please teach me how to feel...

Apparently, the beings in the universe love to teach. And the best way to get toward your goal is to know how it feels to have it; or build an understanding of your goal by exploring and feeling it's various aspects. For instance, if you want to be rich, then it would be a good idea to know the feeling of being lucky. You could say that a lucky person believes in a benevolent universe. That's a nice puzzle piece to have in your picture of wealth consciousness. There are some ways of being and feeling that, because each of our lives are so unique, some may feel as their norm, while others aren't even aware these feelings can exist. These ways of being may be so integral to one person's nature that they wouldn't know how to feel any other way. For instance, the feeling of entitlement that comes with being born with wealth and privilege. Further, these feelings might be so completely out of the scope of another person's normal day-to-day thoughts and actions that they aren't even aware of it.

For example, have you ever looked at another person and were mildly annoyed by how happy or attractive or successful they seemed? Did it seem so far out of your experience that you dismissed their happiness as something that was simply unattainable for you? Now you can say to yourself "Whatever they have, or however they feel, I can feel the same way." You don't need to know their exact state of mind beforehand; you just need to imagine a goal which might involve those states of mind. Then all you need to do is ask for a few nights in a row. When you wake up in the morning of the fourth or fifth day and tune in, you just might have a surprisingly new feeling that helps you understand your goal more clearly Often, just this taste is enough to show you the path, however long, that will lead you to a more expanded and integrated experience of your goal. Then you can take that path until you reach the finish line. By that time, a new goal will certainly have emerged; one that brings even more joyful, peaceful, and harmonious states of mind than you ever thought possible in your life.

When I was younger, I was chronically depressed and didn't even know it. When, as an adult, I began to awaken spiritually, I discovered many ways to uplift myself. I also balanced my spiritual seeking with holistic therapies. After a few years of this, I would happen to look into another person's face and see the expression that I used to see on my own. I knew in that moment that I had come far enough in my development that I would never return to that particular state of mind again. I had learned that lesson and overcome that challenge and had turned the page. Though I was aware that there would still be times of darkness in my life, it would not be the same darkness. I am also sure that in the future, I will look back on myself as I am now in the same way, seeing how far I have come.

ABOUT DREAMS

You have probably noticed that I haven't mentioned dreams. There's a reason. I have found little correlation between what I decide do work on during the night and what dreams I may or may not have. Sometimes dreams are good fodder for a psychotherapist, sometimes only tenuously so, and sometimes just random frustration. They do not seem to relate to the success of the work.

When I do dream, I only pay attention to broader trends. Whatever scenario my dreaming head dreams up, how am I reacting? If I am about to get swallowed up by a tornado, how do I feel about it? Am I just keeping one step ahead? Am I calm or anxious? Am I trying to rescue anyone or do I just keep losing my stuff?

Over the years, the trend I have noticed (and I credit this somewhat to my work with programming my sleep), is that no matter what is going on in my dreams, I don't feel particularly threatened. I may have to handle whatever is happening, whether it is scary or just annoying, and it seems that the confusion ruling my dreams is mostly random and ultimately benign.

Occasionally I will have a lucid dream, and these I will pay attention to. A lucid dream is something I interpret as real information, in whatever clothing it appears. If I have one of these dreams and wake up unsatisfied or feeling unresolved about it, I simply go into my mind and step back into the dream and use every tool in my tool bag to resolve it. Sometimes this can take a while, and it may take practice, too. That's what the snooze button is for.

TAKING THE HELM

When you are ready to put on your captain's uniform and board your very own Magic Nights ship, I recommend these two inaugural journeys as a way to get comfortable on your ship and try out your sea legs. The first is a journey to a peaceful mind:

ITINERARY #2: A SILENT MIND

Imagine moving quietly away from port into a calm ocean on a clear, cool night full of stars. Think of feeling completely safe at the helm of your ship as the sails gently flutter. As it drifts slowly out into the vast night ocean, the moon scatter's its silver light over the soft ripples in the water ahead. The stars twinkle as they crowd the silent night sky.

Love and light, love and light, love and light...

Now set the automatic steering forward gently:

According to free will and for the good of all...

Put on your best captain's uniform.

I call forth my inner wisdom, my divine essence and my authentic self in harmony and   wholeness to give me strength and clarity during my journey tonight...

Invite a couple of your favorite crew members, such as a mascot or power animal and your guardian angels.

Relax in a hammock in the front of your ship and ask the universe to teach you how to feel and experience a deeply silent and peaceful mind:

Please teach me how to have a silent and peaceful mind with perfect clarity and awareness, in the way that is for my highest and best good...

And relax. Repeat this intention and itinerary for at least four nights in a row. And pay attention to how you feel when you awaken in the morning.

Not only is a silent and peaceful mind a wonderful and healthy place to be from time to time, you can place it in your inner tool chest as a skill that can be very useful in certain challenging circumstances:

SILENCE AS A TOOL

In our noisy, round-the-clock world, creating a peaceful, silent mind is a challenge. People meditate to find inner peace with varying degrees of success. Even trying to find it in a natural setting outdoors can be difficult, since the outdoor options are often busy with other nature lovers and sports enthusiasts. Prolonged inner noise can often lead to insomnia, which depresses the body's immune system, creating or exacerbating health problems. Many of us are unable to turn off our inner chatter by force of will alone; and it has never occurred to us that the ability to create inner silence is something we might need to promote a healthy life on all levels.

I never went looking for this kind of silence in my younger years, but one day I found myself having to find it quickly in order to protect myself. I had just begun to meditate and was also mixing socially with some people who were practicing Pagans. Like people anywhere, there were many good ones, many benign ones and a few bad apples. Once I sensed that one of them was trying to influence me using magickal techniques. It felt like a psychic attack, like manipulation and made me angry. I was suddenly having an energetic argument with him. He was telling me what to do and I was resisting. Apparently, he was powerful and practiced at this form of manipulation. I didn't like this game, so I gave him the silent treatment. I clamped my mouth shut in my mind; I shut my thoughts down, one by one. I noticed that every time I would allow a thought to slip through, he would latch onto it, and onto my mind and try to control me. Furious, I persisted in my rebellious stance.

I soon realized that when my mind was silent, he couldn't find me. I could sense him, as his mind was certainly not silent, but I became invisible to him. After a very long ten minutes of shutting off my thoughts, I crossed a mental barrier. Suddenly, it was no longer an effort to be silent in my mind. I was in "quiet neutral" with just a little continued focus. Ah, protection! I was very happy to have discovered this tool. I continued to practice it from time to time so that I would be able to silence my mind at will. I didn't know when I would need it next.

A few years later, I was strolling alone down a sidewalk of an historic town full of homes and buildings from the Revolutionary War era. As I was casually looking at the brick facades, I saw a stately old mansion, set back a bit from the street. I glanced into one of the dark upper windows and I sensed someone looking out toward me. She was very dark, angry and felt dangerous. I guessed it was some kind of dark ghost. Quickly, the ghost caught me looking at her. She immediately attempted to latch onto me like some kind of energetic vampire, or maybe she wanted to possess my soul. I wasn't going to wait around to find out.

I immediately broke the gaze, quickened my step, and started shutting down my mind. I was terrified, but eventually I shut off my mind long enough, and consistently enough that the ghost couldn't find me anymore. When I finally reached the corner, I turned down another street and was finally out of sight, out of range and very relieved.

These days I rarely find the need to defend myself in this way. Now it is more a helpful space to be in. When I find my mind too busy with "should"s and long to-do lists; I stop, sit down and become quiet in my mind. I remember a saying I had picked up somewhere along the line: *"All you have to do is 'be', and the 'do' takes care of itself,"* I silence my mind and "be" for as long as it takes. Typically, just a minute or two later, the "do" will come to me as a idea or instruction that feels perfect in the moment. With that nugget of inner wisdom, I feel I can confidently move on with my day and forward with my life.

DAY TRIPS: WHEN THE STUDENT IS READY

An easy way to practice visualizing inner silence, and also to take the next step of allowing a wise friend to join you in that peaceful place is to.use the phrase, "When the student is ready, the teacher will appear." Imagine yourself in a quiet place, alone in nature. It can be a beach or mountaintop. As far as your eye can see, there are no boats or planes or telephone poles or any other man-made objects.

Then set your safety intention for all to be in love and light, according to free will and for the highest good of all. If you are on a beach, feel yourself sitting on the sand at the shoreline. Feel the the sand between your toes. Listen to the waves. Listen to the seagulls. Feel the wind. When you feel present in that moment and settled, state aloud in your visualization:

When the student is ready, the teacher (or Master) will appear.

Then wait for a few beats and say in your loudest inner voice,

The student is ready!"

Wait and listen as if you are expecting to hear someone's footsteps approach, crunching on the sand. Listen as if you're trying to hear a very faint voice. After a few seconds, usually at least ten, someone who feels good, completely loving and safe may then come and give a teaching. Use your discernment. With time and practice, you will be able to recognize or sense the teacher's message (versus the quicker,louder more insistent voice of your inner fears) and learn how to receive it. When you feel complete, thank them and return to the present.

GETTING TO KNOW YOUR CREW

It is important to have a comfortable understanding and appreciation of the help that is there for you on a non-physical level, no matter whether it is a personification of an idea or a multidimensional being on another plane of existence. Though many of us have been taught to pray to a single god or prophet, I encourage you to get acquainted with the different styles and powers of those crew or guests who accept your invitation to your journey into the night. You may want to begin with getting acquainted with your master guardian angel, then expand your experience with other types of crew.

For instance, I find that journeying with the essence of the divine ascended masters has one particular feel and flavor; you may feel wisdom and blessings and a very loving presence, while journeying with the white whale lodge of peace is a very different experience. When you journey with the whales, you can bring them your biggest problems. The whales, in my experience, are always bigger and more powerful than any challenge you may need to resolve. In addition, if you jump on their backs, the whales may take you on a wonderful journey to the bottom of the ocean for healing and pure joyful play.

BACK TO THE DOCK WITH YOUR TREASURES

When you awaken, allow yourself about ten minutes to revisit your dreamtime circle and thank them for helping you during the night. Ask if there is anything else that would be good for you to learn or know. Then listen for an answer in words, a feeling or a vision. This is when some useful information, or the 'to do' list will be communicated to you. If you have difficulty hearing or receiving information, just request clarity, truth and understanding, and assistance during the day to integrate the work you have done at night. When you feel complete, relax, release and welcome the new day with gratitude.

During the day, pay attention to any feelings or ideas that arise from deep within. Allow your mind to wander to your night's request and think about it without any attachment to results. Take note of any ideas or sudden realizations that may come to you. Do they make sense? Do they feel right? And watch for the answers to your requests. In one form or another, in just the way you can accept them in the moment, and with perfect timing, they will come. If you have great, grand goals, the journey may take years of tiny steps. But if you keep the goals closer to home and easier for your current lifestyle to contain, then results may come to you much more quickly.

THE PORT OF SUPPLY

Water: Love Yourself Completely
Food: Know Who You Are
Fire: Everything is All Right
Air: Surrender
Wood: World Service

The Port of Supply is where you fill your ship with supplies and build a foundation that will support you on your specific journeys. It's like stocking up on basics so that when you find your treasures, you are strong enough to take them home with you and enjoy them. Also, the Port of Supply is somewhere that you can return to when you aren't quite sure what you want, or feel confused and overwhelmed. When you first begin your journeys, I recommend spending at least a few nights gathering each supply before going out on larger adventures.

FRESH WATER: LOVE YOURSELF COMPLETELY

Please teach me how
to love myself completely
Or
Please teach me how it feels
to love myself completely
Or
Please teach me how it feels
to love myself completely
in every cell of my body
and through every level
and aspect of my being

This first request for your night's journey may appear frivolous, but it is truly a foundation. If you don't know how to love yourself, to feel full of love, then there will be little available to offer others in your life. Come from a full place and your efforts will be much more powerful and effective. I recommend setting your course to this destination of self-love for a full week.

When I was first introduced to this concept, it sounded almost silly and I didn't even know how to approach it. I knew that it was important, though, so I asked for another way to understand. The answer I got was "Start with your toes." So I reached down and massaged my toes while saying, "I love my toes completely, I love myself completely," and then "I love my feet completely, I love myself completely," and worked my way up to my head. Also, in the privacy of my office, I made an attempt to mean what I was saying and to enjoy it. It does work. It gave me a more direct and physical feeling of this primal and essential love.

DAY TRIPS: SHOWER POLISH

Treat each day as a ceremony of life – your life. Begin the day with a cleansing shower that will wash away all the dust of the world without and within. Breathe a few deep cleansing and energizing breaths but be careful not to hyperventilate or become lightheaded. Use this private time to nurture yourself, especially all those parts of yourself that you may dislike or ignore or that give you discomfort in any way.

If you are a man, imagine that your body is a priceless exotic sports car. Your hands are gently polishing its finish to a deep luster and are energizing its powerful engines of muscle and bone. Don't miss a single spot. If you seem to see evidence of aging or imperfection, give those areas special care and attention. Remember and encourage your body's miraculous inner powers of self-adjusting and self-healing.

If you are a woman, imagine your hands as the best trained massage hands in the world as you cleanse in an honoring gentle way. Your fingers have the feathers of angels extending from them, which reach inside of your body to gently energetically massage your joints, inner tissues and organs and soothe your inner being. Pay special attention to your breasts, feet, hands and joints and any part of you that you don't like or appreciate. Let the water rinse away any discomfort or stress and imagine it going right down the drain. Step out of the shower like the goddess Venus rising from the ocean.

How you feel is more important than how you might look in the mirror. In a few days or weeks, you will find yourself feeling better and more comfortable in your body. Aches and pains may lessen. You may be inspired to care for your body in other healthy ways. As you honor and nurture yourself in your shower time, prepare to be pleasantly surprised at how others may respond to the new you.

When you are sure you have the feeling and the experience of loving yourself completely, then you may also ask to *know how it feels to be loved completely by the universe.* This will create a wonderfully balanced flow of love in your life which will make it much easier to love and be loved by those around you.

FOOD FOR THE SOUL: KNOW WHO YOU ARE

Please teach me how to know who I am.

This is another foundational concept, like food supplies. It may require a bit of soul searching during your waking hours so that you can figure out your true passions, talents and abilities. Your goal is to build a confident self-image that becomes deeper and more resilient so that it can withstand the pressures of the limiting societal norms and assumptions. Discovering, and knowing Who You Are will most likely be a lifelong process that builds and strengthens slowly over the years. Setting your goal and then moving forward with an image or feeling, can create a safe haven in this fast-changing world.

A WARM FIRE: EVERYTHING IS ALL RIGHT

Please teach me how to feel and know that everything is all right.

Here is where you repair and refresh your safety supplies and hard goods. You want your journey to be as comfortable and worry-free as possible. If you don't stop for these supplies, your crew will remind you. Many a morning, as you tune in and ask for your daily advice, you may simply be given the feeling or reminder that "Everything is all right." Over the years, this will build a solid confidence in the benevolent nature of the universe.

Hobnobbing with ethereal beings has gradually taught me that I am much more than the localized consciousness in my physical body. I am a soul with value to the universe. No matter what I look like, or if I live or die, this will not change. It's a nice feeling. It helps me to move forward and take certain calculated risks, knowing that everything I do counts and that my value is guaranteed by those who know me for the divine soul that I am. If nothing else, their response to my questions and challenges is, at its most basic, "Everything is all right; we are here for you."

I recommend building this feeling within you as a baseline. This will help keep you from being incapacitated by short term fears, and it will keep you and your crew focused on your more positive, long term goals.

JUST BREATHE: SURRENDER

I surrender all levels and aspects of my body, soul and being into divine love and light for healing, harmony and balance, for my highest good and the highest good of all.

I surrender my fears and anxieties.I surrender my anger and resentments. I surrender my feelings of disappointment into divine love and light.

To be healed and transformed as is for my highest and best good and the highest good of all.

You are on your ship and just feel like collapsing in the hammock on deck and staring at the sunset. Think about that part of yourself, that unused part of your brain that knows so much more about who you are and what you are capable of. This journey is one of surrender, so as tired as you may feel, it is good to know that there is a part of you that is always strong. Start by putting on your captain's dress uniform, however you would like to imagine it, and acknowledging your inner wisdom and your connection to the divine spark of creation within that got you where you are now. Call forth in wholeness and harmony that part of yourself, which is your authentic self, your inner wisdom, your divine essence, and your inner God or Goddess.

When you invite your crew, you will probably want only your closest and most trusted advisors, helpers, healers, and guides, so keep the invitation list short, but still open to whomever is best for you in the moment. I would invite my master guardian angel, a couple of my most trusted power animals, and perhaps a few helpers, healers, and guides who are perfect for my highest good in the moment. Of course, be sure to thank them from your heart for coming to be with you.

Next, surrender. Since you effectively surrender each night when you go to sleep, this shouldn't be too uncomfortable. By now, you have protected yourself and have set an intention for your highest good. Humility is also important to remember. I used to remind myself that humility opens doors, just like gratitude does, while fear or anger closes them. For an even better experience, trust in the non-physical beings who are happy to step in and carry you safely through the night. If you open the doors to your heart and soul, you open the way for good and wonderful things to come into your heart and your life.

As you may have noticed, I sometimes add a few qualifiers to my intention: "...Through all levels and aspects of my being, in all time and space, in past, present and future..." These qualifiers are not required. They are just my way of making sure that some past or parallel life doesn't get in the way of my goals. I believe in covering all the bases I can think of, whether I actually believe in them or not

Once you have taken these steps, relax as much as possible into a place of quiet, complete surrender, humility and gratitude. To make this a little easier, you may repeat the mantra "Thank you, God" until you fall asleep.

In the morning after a surrender journey, tune in and thank your inner wisdom and your crew. Then pay attention to how you feel and ask them what you need to know for the day. You might, as I have, come to understand that surrendering to your highest good can make your life path just a little bit smoother, bring along just a few more opportunities and give you that sense of gentle relief that helps you regain momentum toward your goals in life.

WOOD: BUILDING GOOD WILL

You may ask why a service journey would be in the Port of Supply. It's simply because sometimes things tend to feel a little out of balance when every nighttime intention is, "I want" this or that. To bring your life back into balance, and to encourage more and better help from your crews, it's always wise to offer some kind of world service. Think big when taking these journeys. Think global. The more energy you can channel to the universe, the more energy you will be able to receive from it as well and channel it toward your personal goals. So, gather your crew and go to a disaster zone, or a part of the earth you would like to help in some way.

A while ago, I made a few journeys to help with the an oil spill in the Gulf of Mexico. I had a wonderful time with the whales and the energies from the universe, and assisted the world leaders that were coming in to help heal the waters and the leaks. I felt that I was contributing to a solution from my heart. It also helped me to move through the waves of global panic that come with these kinds of events.

But as new earth challenges arise, you may find it just as helpful to ask the Earth to guide you to where she needs the most help in the moment. Then you will feel your work is perfect and effective and timely. Eventually you may come to understand and feel how powerful your thoughts and intentions can really be. You can feel like you are doing your part to save the earth. And as you do, you may find and feel that there are many others out there with you, creating a beautiful new world for all of us.

ITINERARY #3: WORLD SERVICE JOURNEYS

If you have a desire to give back and to help the earth and all her creatures, spend the night on a World Service Journey. Like a dripping pure sacred water gently into a pond, the waves of energy this will create will go around the world and come back to you magnified and full of gratitude from all you have helped. If you spend just one night a week in service, you will help to keep your life in balance and bring more energy to your personal goals. I also recommend inviting lots of friends and crew, perhaps even additional ships full of crew. Remember that when involving others in your journeys, either as helpers or receivers of energy, it is important to stress that it is according to free will and for the good of all, and given in love and light. And, as a special safety, do not consciously choose the receiver of your energy. They may not want it or need it. That being said, these journeys can be especially wonderful and surprising.

Just before you go to sleep, say these Magic Nights words to your inner being and the universe. Say them in your mind or out loud. Say them as many times as you like until you feel complete.

In love and light, according to free will and for the highest good of all, I now call forth my authentic self, my divine nature, my inner wisdom and my higher mind to my sleep and dreaming time tonight. As I am that I am, I open my heart and offer my most loving gentle help to Mother Earth and whomever most needs and welcomes it this night.

I invite the most perfect and powerful helpers, healers and guides in the whole universe to assist me in those who most welcome and need it this night. I invite (your choices for the night)

75

According to free will and for the highest good for all. In love and light. Thank you.

In the morning, make special time to feel and listen for your results, then thank yourself and any crew you may have invited. As you become better at receiving your inner wisdom and guidance, the information might surprise you with it's specificity. And even though you have no proof of your efforts, you will feel good about yourself, and better about your world.

PRACTICE, PRACTICE, PRACTICE

In order to enhance your full understanding of each concept, you may repeat the words of your request during the day. When you have a moment to allow your mind to wander, let it wander to your intention. Take time to notice how your body feels as you say the request in your mind. Say it like you mean it, even if you are only saying it silently. Charge it with energy and feel the words resonate through your entire body.

Your goal is to fully understand and truly know what it feels like to have achieved your intention. If you don't think you understand it yet, or know it, you don't. You'll know when you know. Knowing is a deeper understanding that comes not just from your mind, but also from your soul and spirit.

MOVING ON

After about a week, or until you feel satisfied that you know your first intention or concept, take a couple of nights to have a surrender and a world service journey, then move on to the next intention. In a few weeks, you will find your own rhythm of learning and knowing when to move on. You may receive more instructions, or different ones than those I have introduced here. However, remember these foundational journeys to the Port of Supply and use them when you feel that you are no longer moving forward toward your goals and in your life.

JOURNEYS TO HEALTH

HEALTH DEFINED

Physical health is not just about being out of pain. Health is about quality of life in all stages of life. It's not just about the right doctor or hospital; it's about using our resources, including the Internet, to make informed choices and create our own health and wellness support system. It's about taking off our blinders and looking at all the available options.

Along with hospitals, doctors and medication, we can now, without apology, go to our chiropractor, acupuncturist, or other holistic healers. We can visit any number of health food or vitamin stores for a vast array of choices in herbs, supplements, homeopathics and other nutritional support. The use of holistic techniques and concepts is now more commonly seen throughout the health industry. For instance, hospitals are remodeling to create a calmer, more peaceful environment and in-home care is becoming more popular as people understand how a comfortable, supportive and personal environment can allow for a more natural and harmonious result. The body is physical, energetic, emotional, mental, and spiritual. Every cell is interconnected with every other cell in multiple ways.

Acupuncture is a wonderful illustration of this interconnection. A technique thousands of years old, it focuses on the body's energetic pathways and connections. Each part of the body can be a roadmap to every other part. Have you ever seen a chart for foot reflexology, or iridology, or the acupuncture points on the ear? The foot contains a connection and portal to every part of the body, as does the ear, the eye, the hand, and the head.

Also illustrated by acupuncture methods, the various organ systems are linked to emotional states. Anger tends to reside in the liver, resentment in the gall bladder, grief in the lungs. Our connection to spirit is located generally at the top of the head, and our connection to the earth, or physical support, is located at the base of the spine. Acupuncture, along with its ability to treat pain and physical dysfunction, acknowledges the connection between the physical, the energetic, the emotional, the spiritual, and the mental. How you feel can be a large part of how you heal. Magic Nights can create the feelings, then inspire you to do the work during the day to integrate those feelings and create a new way to care for your body.

The tools I give you for Magic Nights can easily and safely be part of your daily life's tool chest and can complement your program for health and wellness Fortunately, this is an easy process, can be practiced anywhere that allows for rest or reflection. It can, with commitment and patience, lead to a new vision of self-help health that has the ability to draw from unlimited resources and offers an unlimited scope of benefits.

JOURNEYS TO A GOOD NIGHT'S SLEEP

In the chapter "The Magic Words," I told the story about my first experiences programming my sleep. Where at the time I was just trying to make four hours of sleep feel like eight, now I can define whether my sleep is for deep rest, deep healing or moving toward my goals. The intention below is how my journeys to my own Magic Nights began.

First create your safety and make sure your ship is ship-shape. Next put on your captain's uniform of all of your highest aspects, then set your intention for the night:

Please bless me tonight with a deep, restful and healing sleep, so that when I awaken in the morning at the perfect time, I will feel completely rested, completely refreshed and ready for the new day. Thank you.

JOURNEYS TO HEALTH AND WELLNESS

Since our bodies are miraculous and extremely complex organisms, it can be difficult to feel confident as we choose our path to health. Even the best doctors don't always know the root cause of a problem. In many cases, we will follow their advice by merely treating symptoms and crossing our fingers that the body's innate healing mechanisms will take care of the rest. This means that when you choose a healing path for your nighttime journeys, it is a good policy to first ask for general good health, then add a request to heal a specific area or health challenge.

Some of us want to reclaim that vibrant, carefree feeling that we remember from our days as young adults. However, since our bodies continually learn new things and adapt to our current world, it might not be the best plan to ask to feel just as you did when you were young. That could be interpreted as regressing to a previous state, which is probably not for your highest good right now.

To begin, think about what the word "healthy" means to you. Does it mean freedom from dependence on medicines? Does it mean freedom from physical limitation? What would you do if you were completely healthy? What sports do you like? What would you do if you weren't at all concerned about your body's ability to function perfectly as you pursue your joys and passions? Which of the following words would you choose to describe your ideal state of health?

Healthy, Happy, Whole, Balanced, Harmonious, Resilient, Beautiful/Handsome, Graceful, Athletic, Strong, Brilliant

I recommend beginning with a request for overall health, then you may add a focus on a particular health challenge you may have. As for all intentions, give this intention at least four nights in a row to begin to work its magic. If you don't feel complete, take a few nights to rest normally, then begin again:

Please teach me how it feels to have a healthy, whole, strong and resilient body that is graceful, fun and attractive...

or

Please bless me now with a healthy whole balanced strong and resilient body, in the way that is for my highest and best good and for the highest good of all.

And add:

I now invite the highest and best --- doctor in the universe to support deep and harmonious healing of my ... in the way that is for my highest and best good.

You can also request to go to a spa or health retreat setting of your choice. Metaphysical books often mention that there are many such healing temples in the other realms and on other planets. Each seems to focus on a particular area of health and wellness. You might want to research these and use some as examples or imagine one of your own. You may find, in addition to feeling healthier and more at ease in your body, that nighttime journeys to health may result in inspirations that will help you to find more appropriate healers during the day, and at the right price.

Once I found myself feeling uncomfortable in my body and prisoner to an odd collection of vague symptoms. To shift out of this fear and malaise, I began asking for physical health and wellness every night. By the fifth day I felt better, and more help had arrived. There was a monthly gathering of healers nearby that I had been attending. That night one was requesting volunteers to be his test subjects for a therapeutic technique he was studying. He needed a certain number of case studies that qualify for certification. And he refused all payment! It was just the kind of health support that I needed at the time. It was fun, easy and helpful and I was very grateful for the experience.

Sometimes a word will surface in my mind that directs me toward a perfect solution. During this same week of asking for health, my inner wisdom kept repeating the word "amygdala". I knew it was a part of the brain and asked my CranioSacral therapist during a session to check my amygdala. I found out that many of the physical stresses that I had been having were directly related to the ability of my amygdala to function properly. It was essential to get this addressed for proper healing, and my Magic Nights had given me the key.

These results are similar to the Magic Store idea that I speak about in the chapter on Wealth. When you know how to ask for what you want and be open to what the universe sends you, you will learn to expect it to appear right in front of you at the perfect price or in a single perfect word to guide you forward to your goal.

DAY TRIPS: WALKING TALL

Have you ever noticed your own posture and movement habits by passing a plate glass window? Have you ever been able to describe someone else's state of mind just by watching them move? Do they hunch out of protecting their heart or having a muscle imbalance? Are they muscle bound but inflexible and stiff? How does someone who is unhappy move compared with someone who is happy, successful or creative? When a famous actor moves through a scene, what does this say about their character? How does their body movement help tell the story?

If you would like to retrain your movement to reflect who you would like to be, or like to be perceived as, there is a way to do this using a treadmill and some mirrors or reflective surfaces. With the approval and guidance of an appropriate health professional, use my example below to create your own new moves for your new life:

One day, I stepped onto the treadmill at the gym and found myself looking at my reflection. It told me very quickly that I needed to find a way to move differently – to move the way I wanted to be perceived: as a healthy, graceful, intelligent, creative professional. Using my training as a dancer and therapist, I went to work on myself. A few half-hour treadmill sessions later I was seeing good results; good enough to put in my own life's tool chest, and good enough to share.

First I set the speed at an easy pace and the pitch up just a little in order to emulate normal motion. I had read in a runner's magazine that a pitch of 1.5 created a more normal use of the leg muscles than a flat surface. And it softened the heel strike just a little, which took pressure off of my knees and hips. Once I was satisfied with the machine's settings, I drew from my training in movement from years of ballet lessons. I made myself feel taller, lengthening my neck and pretended someone was pulling up the hair on top of my head like a marionette. I lifted my upper chest and relaxed my shoulders.

Then I turned my focus to my spine and torso. I remembered how important it is to create a strong foundation. I tightened my deep abdominal muscles for support and moved my arms and legs freely from that core foundation. When I was learning Tai Chi and Kung Fu, they stressed, as in ballet, that all movement should be initiated from the deep pelvic muscles and abdominal muscles. My gait motion began with a contraction of my abdomen that twisted my hips, and like a spiral outward motion, my legs followed. My arms naturally balanced that motion. I scrutinized my movement in the mirrors and the blank TV screen in front of me.

I moved my focus further down to my legs. I made sure that they were swinging from my hips freely and easily, and felt balanced from side to side. I walked at a lively but easy pace. I imagined my movement was like a graceful machine, focusing on form rather than speed, distance or time. If I was tiring and felt my form slipping, I adjusted the settings to a slower pace for a few minutes.

I made sure that my head remained as level as I could manage, resisting the tendency to bounce up and down with my gait and listened to the sound of my feet hitting the tread. I knew that a pounding sound also meant a pounding on my joints. I continued to move as fluidly as possible, keeping my core strong, my spine long and erect, and feeling my energy and my breath move gracefully through my body.

Next I thought of some role models for movement; perhaps models, or actresses, or dancers. From some runway modeling training I had in my twenties, I remembered to keep my chest up, hips forward and long arms and legs swinging gracefully. I also thought of famous actresses that had the look and motion I admired and would suit my body type. And I didn't want to forget the grace and ease of a dancer's motion.

I didn't want to neglect my feet and hands either. I pretended I was wearing $500.00 high-heeled shoes (that were magically supremely comfortable) so that my feet would move attractively, and I energized my legs so they felt prepared to break out into an exuberant run at a moment's notice. I also made sure my hands were not curled up like claws. I stretched and lengthened my fingers as I walked, swinging my arms as if they were long and weightless.

If you are a man, your role models and walking style would be different: perhaps an actor or athlete or cowboy. Do you seek a competitive edge in your favorite sport, or are you the intellectual type, wishing to create a persona of brilliant creativity and success. Or do you want it all? Would you choose to be a lion, cheetah or panther? Big cats are not only strong, but flexible, graceful and ready to spring into action at any moment. They are also at the top of the food chain and their confidence shows.

Re-training your movement style is something you can think about anywhere you are. But the treadmill is a great place to begin. It takes away many of the distractions that a walk in another setting would present. So that the next time you pass that plate glass window, your reflection will tell the story you want it to tell: confident, graceful, strong, intelligent, successful, stylish, happy...

A BUM KNEE

Some time after my first experiments with night work, I had stressed my knee by running on an uneven surface, and it was a little sore and cranky. It wasn't bad enough to see a doctor, so I decided to see if the Magic Nights crew could help me heal it properly. Every night for a week I invited in all my usual guides, helpers and healers, and I also invited the best most powerful, most perfect knee healer for me in the universe. I asked them to be with me during the night, healing my knee perfectly and harmoniously for my best good. A week later, my knee was almost completely healed. The night workers had done their job and it was well on its way to a perfect result.

I have subsequently used the night work on many of my aches and pains. It's a good way to get the healing process going, even though in many cases I also see one of my friends who is a qualified professional. I have concluded that doing the night work sets up the area of complaint for a better healing result and gets the process moving in the right direction so that the doctors or therapists have a much easier time when I finally do let them treat me directly.

Being a trained therapist myself, and having spent many years without health insurance, I have been reluctant to run to doctors and have found many wonderful healer friends and many ways to heal myself, treat myself and save a lot of money on medical and dental bills. I've found that it's good to know when it's appropriate to see a professional, but also very important to to use every means at my disposal to educate myself and support myself in getting the best possible result in my healing.

As an example, a cosmic healer that I recently discovered is Dr. Lorphan of Sirius. I was told he was a kind of healing gatekeeper as the head doctor in a cosmic hospital or healing academy called the Great White Lodge of Sirius. He would know the perfect clinician or therapist for whatever ailed me. I put his name into my Internet search engine. Sure enough, he appeared in multiple listings.

I imagined a quiet, wise and warm presence much like the wise menI had read about or seen in movies. But who was I to dismiss Dr. Lorphan just because I couldn't prove he existed. He might just be helpful in more than one way. Maybe he could teach me a healing technique or two, if I asked nicely.

No matter who you envision as your helper or healer, the only important thing is, at the end of the day, do you feel better? Are you getting results in a way that feels right?

JOURNEYS TO HELP WITH EXERCISE AND SPORTS

I am a naturally sluggish person. Though I do enjoy being in good shape, it takes a lot of effort for me to get the ball rolling in that direction. Once I am in the groove of working my muscles, it's easy. After a couple of weeks my body begins to crave the exercise, but sometimes getting myself motivated to start an exercise program is seemingly impossible. To address that problem, I have from time to time resorted to the night work. I ask all my helpers healers and guides to help me get into a strong, healthy, and graceful physical place, and I ask them to motivate me to work on it a little more.

Though I have asked to have workouts during my sleep, I have found that I don't sleep so well. I wake up exhausted instead of rested! Instead, I ask for motivation. That way, when I wake up in the morning, I actually feel like putting on all that spandex and moving my body. Luckily, just asking for general health or honoring your body in other ways like doing the Love Your Body shower meditation will contribute to your motivation toward healthy activities as well.

This leads to the possibility of other helpers. Perhaps you are an athlete and would like some training during your sleep. It has been proven that it is helpful to practice a sport by visualizing it. Athletes use this technique while on long trips. Some words that might be useful are: *grace, coordination, harmony, ease, focus, and confidence.*

THE ELIXIR OF LIFE

Please teach me how it feels to taste the elixir of life, in the way that is for my highest and best good right now.

During the early 1990s I studied for a few years with Sondra Ray, author and spiritual seeker. It was my very good fortune to have had the opportunity to attend a seminar she led called Unlimited Life. During the seminar we were introduced to the idea that, the more evolved we became spiritually, and the more we healed old wounds, the more we could become conscious choosers of our physical experience of life. Ultimately, on some level we choose how we live, how long we live and how we die.

This idea was liberating in that we were given the sense that we, and not some outside force or fate, decided the course of our lives. It also included full responsibility for the results we created in our lives every day. Though it seems that this is a much more common idea now, it was still new at that time, and Sondra had a wonderful way of making sure the idea became securely woven into our everyday lives through lectures and processes.

I was happy to realize that I had the power to choose how I lived. I had the power to choose *"Easy and Pleasurable"* or "Challenge and Lessons Learned." I knew that the decisions and patterns deeply embedded in my unconscious mind had an enduring influence on my life, but there was a way, drawn from ancient Eastern texts and modern psychology, to re-pattern myself and create the life I chose in time.

We were introduced to ancient, and not so ancient, Eastern masters who had complete control over their physical bodies. They seemed something like the prototypical guru sitting cross-legged in the lotus position somewhere on top of a mountain in the Himalayas.

We were introduced to the idea of raising our "frequencies" above mere joy, into bliss and, eventually, ecstasy. I also heard the phrase "the Elixir of Life." I wanted to experience this elixir and asked the universe for a sample. The universe provided a taste for me but also gave with it the encouraging thought that, in time, I could have more and more. I could incorporate more bliss, ecstasy, and unlimited life into my definition of how life is for me every day. This was a very high mountain, but my goat-like self relished this challenge. I set my sights on the top and began to move forward, one step at a time.

The elixir came not in the form of a fabled Fountain of Youth, nor in some mind-altering drug, but in the form of a vision and the feeling of a single drop of honeyed bliss on my lips. When I felt its effect on my being, I knew that unlimited life, physical immortality, and pure creative physical choice were possible. Just concentrating on the thought of the elixir and remembering its sweetness brings back the memory and the power.

I encourage you to ask for a taste of this elixir of life for yourself—a taste of what is truly possible and an understanding that what is possible may be so much better than we can imagine for ourselves. God has dreamed it with so much beauty and magnificence and gentleness, like a blossoming flower, and we, as divine creations of God, have the same opportunity to create the flowering of our own life's experience here on Earth.

BEYOND THE PHYSICAL

Life happens, and we want that experience to be fun, wonderful, and productive, but physical death also happens. It must be acknowledged as another part of our soul's journey. As much as we might desire it, physical immortality may not be in the soul's and spirit's best interest. No matter how much we may want it for ourselves and others, it may be more appropriate to transition to our next phase and into the non-physical universe.

As a healer and chiropractor, I have had the pleasure and challenge of experiencing my clients' journeys through physical challenge and to improved health and wellness. At times, I have to warn a client that the result they envision may not be the outcome of my therapy. No matter how hard I try to achieve their stated goals, their soul and the universe may have other ideas.

Typically, I can sense in a client when a life-threatening condition is present, even if they can't feel it themselves. I have, in a few cases, resolved quietly what I sensed to be cancers or impending heart attacks while the client was merely asking for their achy shoulder to be less achy. This is the job of a therapist such as myself—to treat the whole person and offer a new experience of what life can be like, how good he can feel and how much he is really capable of, given release from the stresses of life. Sometimes though, even I am shielded from the truth of their health. This happened in the case of my own mother.

After years of treatments for various things, my mother finally realized that I was, in fact, a pretty good therapist. She welcomed my treatments, so I did what I could to help her when she asked. Eventually, though, she developed a condition of a bent back, caused by a partially collapsed vertebrae in her spine. This condition required regular sessions to keep her out of pain, and as I would remind her, out of a wheelchair.

A few years ago, she seemed to be struggling with her health. There were also emotional stresses. My brother and his family, whom she had been devoted to over the past seven years, were moving away. She also had a challenging romance which frequently disappointed. Through all of this, I did my best. I worked on her back and her tendency toward anxiety, but there were signs that something else was going on.

She was 75 at the time and having regular checkups. The doctors didn't see anything to worry about, but she was not eating well and began to sleep a lot. I worked and worked on her, and I consulted with friends, but I just wasn't picking up on anything tangible and I wasn't getting great results.

Finally, she went to the hospital for an MRI to check out her digestion. What they found was, as she would later say, shocking: she had advanced, inoperable liver cancer, and I, her daughter and doctor, had not even sensed with my therapeutic touch that something so big was going on. I had not even detected a problem in her liver at all.

In two months, she was gone. During that time, I kept treating her to ease her discomfort, but was powerless to stop the process. It was her process, her soul, her divine path, and nothing I did was going to change that. When I realized I couldn't "fix" her, my true grieving began. When, as her caregiver, and as an experienced therapist with "magic" in my hands, the universe and her soul prevented me from helping her, other than just making her feel more comfortable in her death process, I cried.

In hindsight, I see how it all happened with perfect timing. I had moved back home to the East Coast from California with the idea of being there for her in her later years. I had done a lot of eldercare in California and was not interested in continuing in that profession, and had told the universe that I was not interested being anyone's "Angel of Death," with one exception. I would be available for my own mother, should she need me. When she did become ill a few short years later, there I was, right under her roof and available.

There seemed to be just enough time in her illness for me, my sister, and my brother to handle the details that needed to be taken care of. There seemed to be a way for each of us to help her in our own way, and contribute equally to her process of transition. Everything seemed to be in the nick of time, but everything was perfect. We all did our part. We all felt like we did our duty. She had a great memorial service and her remains are now safely tucked away on the top of my brother's mountain.

We are created so that perfect physical health and unlimited physical life are not always the best answers to our souls journey. I have been blessed in many ways by my mother's passing. As close to the spirit world as I am, I had also been called to help her in her transition to the other side. I cannot judge. I can only be helpful in the best way possible in the moment. In this case, a graceful transition to the compassionate domain of the non-physical, where all is made clear and the ultimate love of the universe is ever present.

Whatever lessons or challenges or wonderful experiences your health and wellness journey may bring, keep asking, keep moving forward and know that, even if your ultimate goal seems not to be achieved, your work is not wasted. Everything counts, every breath and intention and good deed, no matter now the outcome may appear. Your friends, whether in body or spirit, are there for you always, offering to you what you and your spirit call for in the moment. Because they are eternal, you are eternal, and love is the ultimate law of the universe we live in.

JOURNEYS TO WEALTH

* DAY TRIPS: WAVES OF WEALTH
Imagine a great river of a trillion electrons flowing around the planet. In one place, a small stream is diverted away into an imposing structure. There it is translated and transmuted into what we call "money." Deep inside this structure is a dim computer room lit by a wall of glittering screens, which monitor only this small diverted-stream. The minions of the wealthy few busily direct this small stream of trillions of dollars. And those who monitor the minions imagine that this small stream is the means by which they maintain control the planet and everyone on it. But the river of energy is unimaginably powerful, wider and deeper than they could ever understand. The river is not only fed by streams on the planet, but by streams from within the planet, and it is fed by streams of particles from the skies above. The flow has motion and matter, and it is an energy source that doesn't judge those who trawl its depths or come to bathe along its banks. It simply is—abundant, pure and everlasting.

Find a place along the shore of this deep river. Wade into its pure energy and motion. Let your whole body feel the flow. Take in as much as you can. Feel the free-flowing electrons, neutrons, and protons. Notice more beautiful particles that glow with unfamiliar and untold powers. All of them dance in rainbows of harmony around you. You dance with them, recognizing each other as the same, yet unique; all drawn from the vast and infinitesimal mystery of the universe.

Now see that this river of energy flows into a great ocean — an ocean of movement, light, and pure potential. Move toward the water's edge and look over this ocean. Someone puts a surfboard in your hand. Take it and paddle out into those majestic waves. Feel their deep, pure, and powerful energy. As the waves swell, move with them, rise on your surfboard and let it's movement take you. Feel that rush of energy. Enjoy the ride for as long as you can.

When you have absorbed all you can, go back to shore and remember the feeling. Think of that flow of pure potential. What would it take for you to learn to allow and accept more of this abundance into your life? Does it have more to do with what you do, or who you are? How would you bring the vast energy of that ocean through your body and into your life?

STUFF, MEANING, AND MOTION

What is wealth to you? How do you measure it in your life? It is how much stuff you have, or how much money goes in and out of your bank account, or is wealth how you feel?

For most of us, wealth is quantifiable in terms of dollars. Represented most often by the motion of a magnetic strip through a reader, dollars are also the motion of billions of streams of energy flowing through bank accounts. When that flow slows, it seems like everyone suffers. If it were to stop completely, we would stop, frozen in our tracks, not sure where to turn. This is the world we have created.

Imagine that the flow of money did stop. Where is your wealth now? Would you find it in how you feel about yourself and about the world you live in? Is it a feeling of security, of satisfaction, of serenity? Is it a loving family and connection to your community? Is it a sense of purpose and creativity? Is real wealth that happy sigh, an easy movement of breath that says everything is all right?

In a metaphysical sense, wealth could be described as the pure potential of all the collections of atoms that surround us, awaiting our love and attention and guidance; from the rocks and wood that pile up into the shape of a home at our direction, to the plants that transform into a delectable meal with our creative efforts, to the family dog that we shelter and feed, and that in return warms our souls with unconditional love.

ENERGY FOLLOWS THOUGHT

From the time I started studying alternative philosophies, I was told that our true power comes from within. Inside each of us is the potential and the resources to "move mountains" or "change the world, one step at a time." I was told that to tap into this potential and manifest this wealth, we must seek ways to unlock our inner potential. We must dig deep to change our habits of thinking and our inner belief systems. Then the outside world will naturally rearrange itself to reflect those changes. It will also reflect and remind us where opportunities to change still remain.

It is as if whatever you believe about yourself and life, and whatever you protest to be true about life, the universe merely answers with a resounding "YES," and so it shall be, for you. When you say "I can't..." or "maybe for you... " or define life or your job as "hard work" or "a struggle," then the universe merely agrees. You can choose to feel the energy of the ocean of pure potential by standing on the shore and getting beaten up by the powerful waves, or you can get on your surfboard and relish the thrill of riding them. The ocean doesn't judge you either way. On the positive side, the ocean of pure potential has within its depths many wonderful treasures and surprises. No matter what you have imagined would be a great improvement in your life, you can trust that the universe, with its ocean of pure potential, has imagined something much, much better.

DAY TRIPS: SHOWER POWER

To teach your body to allow energy to flow through it more easily, you can use your breath in this simple shower meditation. Then direct that flow toward your desires, just by asking:

Take some time in the shower to cleanse and energize your energy flow. Breathe easily and naturally. Take care not to hyperventilate or become lightheaded during this process and pause during the process if you feel you need to regain your center.

First raise your hands above your head. Inhale slowly and deeply into your lungs and sweep your hands down your body. Imagine you are pulling pure, light-energized air from the sky down through your head and all the way down to your toes, filling your body. When you exhale, relax and release any tension or negative emotion from your body and imagine it going down the drain. Take a few breaths this way until you feel your body is full of energy and light.

Then pull in one more breath of light and energy. Pull it all the way through your body and send it deep into the earth as a gift. Take a few normal breaths until your breathing normalizes and you are comfortable. Then reverse the process.

Reach down and pull golden light nurturing life energy from the earth through your feet and all the way up into your head, using your arms and hands to enhance the flow. On the exhale, release any negative energy or emotion into the water and down the drain. Do this until you feel full, then send one final breath through your body and up into the universe as a gift of gratitude.

Take a few normal breaths. Your energetic core should feel more relaxed, open and clear. You have just expanded your consciousness above your head into the universe and deep into the earth. Settle into this peaceful silence and listen. You now have the powers of the universe at your fingertips.

Imagine that there are particles in the universe that are like stems cells. Some call these particles adamantine particles. You can gather them up from this place of awareness and create feelings and energetic opportunities. You may even hear a benevolent voice ask you what you want.

Whether you hear the voice or not, make your request for the day. Ask for a feeling or a quality, or how you want your day to go. Remember to qualify the asking by stating that it is for your highest and best good and for the highest good of all. Then be still in this expanded place and listen.

After a few seconds, you may feel a lightning bolt of energy shoot down from the universe and pass through you into the earth and into your world. This is the answer to your call. Thank yourself and the universe and whomever else may have been involved in your receiving this gift. Take a moment to feel the moment and appreciate it, then pay attention during the day to see how the feeling manifests for you.

Practice this meditation to experience a form of manifestation, and also to create a clear channel within your energetic core for expansion in many positive ways.

THE HELP

Life gave me an interesting lesson on wealth from the perspective of being "The Help." After I graduated from chiropractic school, I decided that I wanted to live in the mountains. I kept getting this vision of a very tall mountain with the sun shining right at the peak. It called to me. So after pondering the options and asking friends for advice, I moved to Aspen, Colorado. The energy of the earth there fed me. It felt like home somehow. So I found a place to live, got a job, and began to poke around the healthcare scene. At one point I found myself working at an upscale hotel in town. I was supervising in the reservations department and busily booking rooms for guests and groups. Every now and then there was a large banquet in our ballroom. The hotel manager would put out the word—"All hands on deck." As many of us as he could spare would become banquet servers. This hotel was one of the top banquet venues in town, so there were frequently very high-end affairs - filet mignon and lobster and plenty of famous people drifting about. I enjoyed being there, watching people and tasting the atmosphere from that perspective. Though at the same time, I had just gotten my chiropractic license in that state and was seeking opportunities to exercise it. Nevertheless, I put on my server's uniform and began the evening.

I started out as Dr. Polishes Glassware, followed by Dr. Serves Hors d'Oeuvres, Dr. Serves Your Wine and Dr. Gets Your Mink Coat From the Rack of Fifty Mink Coats. While I was at that hotel, I learned great lessons in hospitality that I always appreciate, including some strange things, like which way to lean when the server comes with your dinner plate (the answer would be to the right, since food is served from the left side of the guest and pulled from the right). I also had a few stressful moments when the guests would make assumptions about me based only on what I was wearing and doing at the moment.

101

One night while I was attending to the coat check room, an older woman approached the door and pulled out her coin purse. As she dumped a few quarters into the tip basket she said "That is for your bus ride home, dear." Her condescension stung. Not only did I not need bus fare as I lived across the street on Main Street right in Aspen, I probably had a fancier diploma hanging on my wall than she would ever have. I gritted my teeth, but my mind screamed "That would be DOCTOR Coat Check, to you, madam." I was also thinking of more than a few others working at the hotel that had wonderful talents and abilities that deserved equal respect.

After my work at the hotel was done, I found myself working again as a supervisor. Apparently, I had some aura of authority about me, though my employers didn't know why. This time it was at the front desk of an exclusive golf club in Aspen. That meant that I had the keys to the club, the combination to the safe and was responsible for guest security and tennis lesson schedules, among many other things. I saw more wealthy and famous people. Mostly, the members were as people are: sometimes angry, sometimes nice, sometimes very funny, but frequently in a world all their own. They worried about their party schedules and about their stock portfolios. Though the world they lived in seemed very different than the one I lived in, I began to appreciate the ways in which my life was wealthy as well. And I kept learning.

At one point, it dawned on me that to the wealthy it didn't seem to matter what stuff they had, since they had all the stuff they wanted. What they worried about was who they could trust. Was I going to jump over the counter and ask for their autograph? No. I was better trained than that. Was I stealing the trinkets off their window sills. Certainly not. I had more than enough trinkets of my own that I preferred. Conversely, I was once amazed at the cheap, useless vitamins a particularly sweet and beautiful woman had bought and arranged like precious jewels on her granite counters in her fabulous home where her personal chefs did all the cooking. I was sorry that there was no opportunity to help her in that moment. Every now and then an opportunity would arise to breach the gap. Usually when something simple would flummox them and they would welcome the hand that gently and courteously reached out to assist them.

By that time, I knew that small town, and most of the people in it, pretty well. I had a little place of my own in town, a ski pass for the winter, a hiking buddy for the summer, invitations to parties and nights out on the town. I had the lay of the land and the tools at hand, and was enjoying all the beauty and excitement there. But the ultimate treasure map to my life remained a mystery. Perhaps there was something else I needed at that point in my life that was more important than what I thought I needed. So I asked the universe the biggest wealth question I could think of: How am I really going to make it in this world? After listening for a while, I heard one word very clearly: "Write." Okay. This was new. I was a decent writer in school, but had no particular drive or inspiration to put pen to paper creatively. So I replied to the universe, "Then spoon-feed it to me. Make it easy."

A few days after this cosmic interchange, I did a peace pipe ceremony on my porch. Following the ceremony, I sat down to meditate. Suddenly, behind my darkened lids, I was walking into a dimly lit movie theater. I sat down next to a particular movie star I was fond of and a movie began to play on the screen. I realized what was happening. This was the spoon-feeding I had asked for. So I watched the film, opened my eyes and wrote down what I saw, closed my eyes and watched again until the film had ended. It was apparent that my first writing assignment was to be a screenplay, but I did not get the whole script in the first vision. That vision was just the core story, the idea. Then I went to the library and began to read about screenwriting. About a year and ninety pages later, I moved to Los Angeles. I continued to write, and had enough encouragement along the way to stay hopeful. Surely in the city there would be more opportunities to find my destiny.

STUDYING WEALTH

This was a big town, very unlike the little one I had come from. And the treasure map would look very different. While doing all the paperwork to get my chiropractic license in California, I took some side roads into eldercare, to provide me with housing, and then was introduced to the idea of background acting to fill the gaps in my schedule.

I signed up with the infamous Central Casting. So a few days a week I contracted myself out to work on the many television and film productions in the area. I worked on studio lots and back lots and went to locations. I worked days and night and went to many thrift stores in order to amass the requisite three closets full of cheap outfits in all the right colors (think wallpaper) for background. This experience, up close and in person in "the industry" was invaluable to my screenwriting. I realized I was a pretty decent actor as well. It was grueling, humiliating, exhilarating and lots of fun. Was this a side road or the main road to my best future? It wasn't clear.

My chiropractic license took a long time to finalize. I applied, then was rejected, then battled the State of California to change a regulation so that I could qualify, then applied again. Finally, two years after moving to Los Angeles, I had my freshly minted license in my well-trained hands. Life was interesting and moving forward at a breakneck pace. As fun as it was, it just wasn't bringing in the income I wanted.

Many of us in the healing, creative and metaphysical arenas seem to have difficulty bringing our talents down to earth long enough to create tangible wealth in our lives. Our wealth is carefully nurtured within, but sometimes not evident without. I was no exception.

Eventually I felt I had to put my foot down with myself, and with the universe. I knew from my experiences in my own meditations that there was a part, a facet of my being that had it all figured out. This was a vision of myself as a very wealthy and powerful man, like a great Pharaoh. Unfortunately, somewhere in time between him and me there were patterns and experiences that interfered with that confidence and ability: there was also a facet of my being that felt very much like a monk, trapped in an empty stone cell with all the deep-rooted dedication to poverty, chastity and subservience that came along with those dull brown robes.

I became very annoyed with all these seeming disparities and mustered up the fortitude to do what I knew would get a result. I stomped my foot at the universe and screamed into the sky that I was GOING to solve this problem. I was going to do whatever it took to root out the demons of my financial restrictive patterns, no matter how deep they might be, and I would use every legal and sensible means at my disposal to do so.

I asked around in my circle of friends for help. Prosperity books and programs began to drift into my hands. I went to work. I did all the mantras and meditations. I went to those big over-produced wealth seminars that promised millions. After three or four months of this, I was at a saturation point. I had done everyone else's program to the best of my ability. I realized it was time to do my own. I needed a prosperity program that was from me, for me and customized to my particular needs,background and way of healing and processing. So, in that way that I do, I dug deep and pulled a power tool out of my tool chest. The peace pipe ceremony.

I didn't have a lot of privacy, so I sat down in front of my computer and began a written version of the ceremony (described in Chapter Two). Each week I went through the ritual, and each week an instruction, a perfect phrase came to me. It felt like pieces of a very big puzzle and I had the sense that this was not a quick fix but a long road. I also felt that it was the right road and there was no turning back. I knew I needed to understand, feel and know in my bones the meaning of each phrase. And I had just the tool for this particular job: I would set my intention every night to learn them, just as I had when I commanded myself to sleep well.

The first instruction was to love myself completely. The next, to know who I am. Sound familiar? As the weeks went on and more concepts, more words and phrases of wealth consciousnesses were given, learned and integrated. The wisdom coming through seemed more and more like something that could, and should, be shared. Not only was I headed up a very big mountain, but it seemed I would be building a stairway for those behind me along the way: the stone of luck, followed by the stone of innocence, followed by the stone of feeling like a treasure, followed by the stone of thinking globally. If you would like to know a little of how this felt, you might start as I did, asking the universe to teach you how it feels to be a billionaire. However, Your journey is your own. So, feel free to take an easier and more pleasurable road, knowing that, in the end we will be at the top together, whichever path we choose.

THE MAGIC STORE

One of the ways the universe started to teach me about wealth was giving me the idea of the Magic Store. At that time, I used my habit of going to thrift stores for cheap entertainment and to find fun new things for my closet. I needed lots of clothes for my jobs as a background actor and I didn't have the money to buy them new, nor would I want to since they might get ruined on set. I explored the many thrift stores in the area and found one that seemed to consistently have what I needed at a price I was willing to pay. It occurred to me that if I had needed something, like a certain kind of jacket or other item that thrift stores generally have, and if I thought about it a little, in that casual, common sense way, I found that the very thing I was asking for would appear in my favorite thrift store a couple of weeks later. This particular thrift store then became my "Magic Store."

I began to experiment. I asked the universe, and my Magic Store for specific things like suits, or ball gowns in certain shades, or costumes for work or luggage or gifts, or suits and robes and stoles for my new career as a wedding officiant. For the most part what I requested would appear, but sometimes things would show up in a way that seemed to say that the universe thought I needed something I hadn't known to ask for. Sometimes I just needed something new in my closet, or something just for fun.

One time, to my surprise, my Magic Store had at least twenty pairs of shoes, just in my size. They were brand new, and there were two pairs of each kind in different colors. These shoes appeared on the shoe racks over the next few weeks. To that person who cleaned out her closet, and to a universe that thought I needed some fun and more shoes, I sent my thanks.

Another time, while at work on TV and film sets, I had been noticing and admiring a strange kind of tennis shoe I saw on some of the crew's feet. They had visible heavy springs as heels and were worn by the production assistants and grips who were typically on their feet for sixteen hours a day. They were not just a fashion statement, they were also practical. But they were expensive, so I didn't think much about them until a pair of these shoes appeared in my favorite Magic Store, just like new, in my size, and also in a sensible black. I imagined that whoever bought them didn't take the time to get used to their characteristic wobbly feel, so the shoes ended up at the thrift store. I was happy to pay eight dollars for them, rather than paying the $150.00 that they had cost new. I found that those springs came in handy when I was running or on my feet all day. Thank you, Magic Store.

I had always enjoyed thrift stores, but now I had even more reason to appreciate them and all the people who contributed to that experience. Like a good playmate, I did my best to return the favor. When possible, I would put a bag of goodies at the donation dock before going in the front door. I was recycling in my own way and that felt good.

When I figured out that this was a consistent pattern of asking and receiving, I came up with the phrase Magic Store. Through this experience, I finally understood that the universe tries really hard to give us what we want, and at a price that we think we can pay. All we have to do is ask, show up, and say yes, or say no if we have changed our minds by then. It's our choice. The universe doesn't judge. It just takes pleasure in providing us with what we think we want, and loves it when we have fun, choose and experiment,make more choices and have more fun.

As another example, I once went to an upscale holiday house party in Pasadena, California. These were people of "old money." I was popular that night and the wealthy ladies gushed over my dress. Little did they know that that dress had cost me only fifteen dollars at Goodwill. It hadn't looked like much on the hanger, but the fabric was fabulous gold burnout silk. I tried it on and was pleased it fit me so well. When I brought it to the counter, the other ladies in the store circled around, envious that I had spotted it first.

When I moved away from California, I bemoaned the loss of my favorite thrift store. Where I was moving, thrift stores were few and far between. How would I get what I needed at a price I wanted to pay? Would the universe continue to provide? How much could I dare ask for? I pondered how to expand the Magic Store concept in my life, and the universe expanded at my request. Whatever store I happen to like and visit regularly is now my "Magic Store."

I wondered how far this idea of the Magic Store could go. If I can have a Magic Store, can the store be the whole world? Can I have a Magic World? A Magic Universe? Of course, the answer is yes. The universe always says yes. We have only to ask and know that the universe will do its best to provide. Thank you, universe.

HOW DOES IT FEEL TO BE WEALTHY

My understanding of and capacity for wealth has grown, but there is more to learn. Writing this book and this chapter was an important part of the learning process. I received this message repeatedly. One day while in the early stages of writing this chapter, I felt confused and unclear about what to say. I turned my ideas about wealth over in my mind gently, and then decided to have my mind work on the problem overnight, with the assistance of my usual crew. In the morning I sat down with my coffee, pen and notebook. I felt an answer surface, then come into focus. Suddenly I was in a therapy room, looking at a client on my table. I somehow knew that I was to envision a therapy session much like the ones that I do in my waking hours as a chiropractor. These sessions have a feeling of reality about them. And, as in live sessions, the results can surprise me.

I didn't recognize the man. He appeared to be middle aged and average in every way, but somehow I knew that he was incredibly wealthy. It seemed to seep out of him like a silvery mist. I put my hands on him, and immediately the feelings and sensations began to come. The first sensation was his fortitude. This was not a man that let anyone into his personal space on a whim. But I am a therapist and trained to dive under these defenses. One level deeper, I sensed a web encasing him that was created from the fibers of responsibility and the stresses of success. Then I passed through that web in to a secret place. There, as an egg buried in a soft nest, was a memory, a potential for peace and happiness.that was hidden away long ago. Perhaps this feeling escaped to the surface from time to time but it was not given the attention it deserved.

As I held this small place in my focus with reverence and utmost care, I found my awareness expanding. My crown was among the stars and I was looking down at the Earth, and at my client. From that viewpoint, I felt a moment of universal wisdom and my own divine essence came forth. I understood more. I had the big picture.

A stream of deep desire flowed from the wealthy man. Underneath all the wealth, power, fortitude and stress, he was simply reaching out for a peaceful, unconditional love. He wanted to feel and know that the universe loved and supported him no matter what he or others thought he was.

When he unveiled his deepest desires, he also unveiled his true potential. And, from my larger view, I was given a vision of how the universe saw him, and all of us. The universe saw the depth and breadth of our creativity, our complexity, and our true power. I understood that we are seen, and loved like this in every moment. The universe sees us as multi-dimensional, timeless souls, complete with many lifetimes in many places, and with many different experiences. The universe sees our full, complete potential, uniqueness, and capacity for love, and it wishes only for us to feel its genuine and timeless peace, love, understanding, and support. If we can truly feel and understand our true nature, as the universe sees us, then we can begin to see and accept the gifts the universe has to offer us.

I put my hands on my wealthy client and gave him as much of this energy as I could channel and he could integrate. I was grateful for the vision and for the knowledge that, with the style of holistic therapy that I use, all of my clients can be supported in this way, wealthy or poor, young or old. All people have so much to offer. It is my job as a doctor not just to give attention to their daily health needs, but also to help reveal their deeper, more divine and more powerful potential in every way.

POWER

A study of wealth includes a study of power. Wealthy people have power. Powerful people are not always wealthy in the ways we often interpret wealth, but somehow wealth surrounds them anyway.

Then there's that quote, "Absolute power corrupts absolutely." If we become wealthy, how do we handle the power that comes along with that wealth?

Since "wealth" and "power" are frequently in bed with each other, they can be seen as a romantic couple. Both are highly prized as if they were top models or movie stars, but the relationship dramatic and frequently tumultuous. It can be a whirlwind of selfish intention that causes great suffering for those in its service and those standing close enough to be swept into its unpredictable gusts of energy.

If you were to separate the two into different rooms, wealth might be the female; a chalice, a creative womb of infinite abundance and potential. Power, in another room, would be the male with his ability to move and channel that abundant energy. He takes the wealth, adds his force and manifests that potential into form, affecting his environment and everyone within his influence.

Power can seen as a tool that uplifts, or a weapon that destroys. Wielded by someone with deep-seated fears or low self-esteem, power can manifest as an addiction to dominate and control others. Like a dark elixir, it can be highly addictive, becoming an end in itself. If power is guided by love, the greater the power, the more gently it must be offered in order to protect those within its influence. Then it can serve to lift them up and ease their suffering.

Like the sun, power could easily consume us, but instead it offers life, beauty, and warmth from a perfect distance. It gives freely and also allows us the freedom to choose our own paths, our own lessons and our own ways to discover its embrace.

Wealth is the ability to create energetic potential. It is the size of your ship. Power is the ability to move that energy and the design of your sails or engines. How big is your vessel? Is it a tall ship with many beautiful sails, a yacht, a tanker, or a speedboat? What kind of crew do you want to invite to help you reach your destinations? Most important, how do you want to feel when you are at the helm? Do you want to *have* wealth and power or *be* wealthy and *be in* your power?

JOURNEYS TO WEALTH

What are the magic words to set you on your journey to true wealth. that is perfect for you right now? What are the feelings, understandings, and knowledge that will move you closer to your goals and help you feel like a wealthier person in every part of your life? Are there things about wealth that you don't even know that you don't know?.

I know with certainty that this is true in my life. When I first began receiving the words and phrases to study on my journey to financial abundance and freedom, I quickly realized that many of the concepts and feelings that I was given were completely foreign to me. I imagined that very financially wealthy people must define and interact with life in certain ways that I could not even fathom, and that they probably weren't even aware of this.

Asking to be introduced to these feelings at night was a wonderful and perfect way to learn these new feelings and ways of being. I understood from all of my studies that there was a part of me that already had that knowledge hidden deep within my body and psyche. There was an inner wise person, an inner divinity that had the big picture. Now I had an even better way to reach those hidden treasures and bring to the surface those places of feeling, knowing and understanding would help me reach my goals in life.

These magic words and phrases and concepts were sometimes simple and complex and were particular to the place, time and who I was at that moment. Yours will be, too. What words and images come to mind when you think of wealth? Freedom? Purpose? Creativity? Productivity? Enjoying the love of family and friends? How would you finish the phrase: "I feel okay about my life and sense of wealth when I..." Would the answer be to have your bills paid on time, or to have a certain amount of money in your

112

checking account? Would that make you feel that everything was okay? Or would it be to have a good job, or in this economy, have a job at all? Would it be to own your own home? Where is that line that, when crossed, throws you into fear about money? It's different for everyone, and like a set point, the objective is to change it.

I used to be okay with making $43.00 for a day's work and keeping my bank balance just above zero. I could live below the poverty line and hobnob with wealthy people at fancy parties with grace and ease. Now my set point, my comfort level with my own finances, has risen a bit. Currently I live simply in some ways and extravagantly in others. I spend my energy and money on healthy food, musical creativity and cameraderie, on travel, writing and on spiritual expansion. I still go to consignment shops from time to time for fun clothes and wonderful surprise finds. In my life, I prefer to feel that I am traveling the path of destiny and am not just wandering the roads of fate and karma. But, of course things change all the time and I have learned not to try to predict my life very far into the future. There are still many magical adventures and wonderful worlds to discover waiting out there for me that I can't even imagine right now. As I said, I know the universe has imagined it so much better than I have, so I trust and eagerly anticipate each bend in the road and each change in the winds.

Think of your personal journey to wealth like a spiral ladder that you are climbing. As individual as your own DNA, this ladder changes as you rise up each step. You may come around and find yourself revisiting some concepts and ideas of wealth in different places on your ladder. You may also add to, rebuild or reactivate sections or strands of your DNA. After all, in some new age circles it is generally agreed that humans are actually supposed to have 12 active strands of DNA. We are really supposed to be much smarter and more capable than we are now. Just think of how that would feel? If this, or something like it, is true, are these inactive strands or segments being activated by your Magic Nights journeys?

ITINERARY #4: A BRILLIANT IDEA

Everyone can be a superhero. Just tap into your whole brain every night for a brilliant idea or two. This is a fun way to experience how Magic Nights can take advantage of your innate intelligence and simultaneously explore the vast intelligence of the universe.

At first, I recommend keeping your request general by asking merely for a brilliant idea. Then you can add more fun and function by qualifying your request: How do you want your brilliant idea to feel and operate? Do you want it to be fun, easy and profitable? Do you want it to be a great conversation starter? Do you want it to empower you or the whole planet, or both?

Some Magic Words to tease your brilliance out of your brain could be:

Please give me a brilliant idea that is for my highest and best good and the highest and best good of all. I would like this idea to feel (pick some qualifiers) fun, easy, elegant, brilliant, and empower myself and others.

You may soon find other people telling you how smart or brilliant you are. It's a good sign. Pay it forward!. Tell them just to ask for their own brilliant idea every night, just before bed...

GET A JOB

When I was just beginning to write this book, the universe provided me with a few months of relatively stress-free income to focus on the first attempt to get my ideas organized and on paper. However, this seemed to create some concern among my friends and family. They gently hounded me; When was I going to get a job? After a while I did begin to get a little stir-crazy, so I began to hunt more seriously for "a job." Trawling the Internet, I discovered a new networking and self-help group called the Holistic Job Seekers Meetup. It sounded interesting and fairly appropriate to my task. More importantly, it might give me information and ideas for this book

At a local library I was greeted by one of the creators of the group. She was a dynamic, experienced and unemployed human resources manager. She was accompanied by others of her credential as well as a random clutch of job-seekers. We enjoyed sharing great information about the employment scene, how to market yourself, internet networking and resumes.

While there, I was reminded about putting your best foot forward by dressing for the job you want, not the one you have. As I looked around at people's personal presentation, some were not very attentive to their appearance and some were solidly in the suit world. I, on the other hand, showed up doing my impression of a Hollywood creative director - tailored but relaxed in nice jeans, a crisp collared shirt and fabulous blazer. I wasn't wearing $500 shoes, but the general theme was there—successful, polished, creative, independent. I was secretly relieved that I had actually learned something over the years from my very tailored professional, mother, and also from my work in the entertainment industry. I had stood in front of many wardrobe trailers to pass inspection and sat in many chairs getting my hair and makeup done for all kinds of roles as an extra. These experiences had, for the most part, counteracted my natural inclination toward a much more bohemian look. So far, so good.

Another idea that came forward was a little bothersome. We were asked to estimate our worth as if we were affixing a dollar figure to our foreheads. It was a given that certain professions had certain pay scales. I ran through the numbers which might be attached to my own forehead. Lacking a clear answer, I took a deeper look. What was I worth, really? How much did I believe I was worth? Did I believe that I didn't deserve a better wardrobe than the discount stores provided? I did balance that thriftiness by my choice to eat expensive, healthy, organic foods. Did the universe have any limitations? Was it alright by the universe to live simply in some ways and feel extravagant and wealthy in others?

Certain aspects of my childhood hadn't encouraged a sense of self worth. Though I had come a long way, I knew some of those old fears and old assumptions were still hiding deep within me. It was time to ask that question, both when I went to bed and during the day: What am I really worth? I really wanted to understand from a larger perspective and feel my worth on a deeper level. So I sent out the invitations that night and made my request.

Within a few days, the answer came perfectly as a phrase that I had used for others but not myself: I am worth a fortune. I didn't really feel it in that moment, but the universe thought I was worth a fortune and wanted me to understand. Obviously, I needed to follow with nightly request to understand this more fully.

I am always amazed at the perfection of the concepts and phrases that come to me when I ask and then listen. The universe knows just what to say in a way that I will understand. It knows just how far I can go in the moment and always answers my questions gently and quickly. Part of my wealth is that I have allowed and developed this support system that is ready and waiting for me. At this point, I don't even have to sleep on it. As soon as I ask, "Teach me how it feels to…, the answer is given.

ASK AND YOU SHALL RECEIVE

I have also found that I should be careful what I ask for, because it often shows up very quickly—so quickly in fact that I am unprepared for its arrival and then can't decide if it was really what I wanted after all. It's not usually big things like winning the lottery, but instead things that I feel are normal to ask for in my life, that are within my current comfort zone. A new printer with all the features I think I need at a great price, or some wonderful free advice for my business. Each step of my journey is supported, each request granted in some way. And though I still have learning and growing to do, the universe keeps offering love and abundance in all the ways I will allow. I think it's a pretty good quandary to be in.

DAY TRIPS: WEALTH AS LOVE IN MOTION

Look within. Where does your wealth lie? How does it flow through your life? How do you measure it and how do you measure up? Take a moment and feel the stream of abundance in your life. Feel the warm presence of the sun, and the joy of the infinitely numerous star blessings raining down from the universe upon you. Touch that inner knowing of Who You Are and the exquisite expression of your divine uniqueness. See that divine essence of You flow out as a blessing into the stream of life.

Watch it flow out into the ocean of pure potential and create a wave of goodness that grows larger and larger. Feel the wave travel across the ocean and all the way around the world. See the lights of all the ones that it washes over grow bright with the joy of its blessing. As the wave comes around the world and back to you, it lifts you up gently and returns to you the gratitude of all those that it has passed over. You are an infinite abundant gift of the universe; to the universe. Do you feel it?

JOURNEYS TO LOVE

LOVE AND FREEDOM

Relationships between people are complicated and multileveled and extend over space and time. They are so valuable to us as human beings on so many levels, that the lessons we learn are worth more than gold. In my own relationship challenges, I have gathered some rules and tools that I hold fast to.

First I remember that I am human, driven by instinctive needs and desires that may overpower any rational thinking I may be attempting to employ in the moment. These survival mechanisms have been operating deep inside our brains since the times before we were even considered human. One is personal physical survival. These days we frequently associate this drive to survive with money. Another instinct is the survival of the species. This could be seen as the messages arising deep from within our DNA that cry for its perpetuation; messages that inspire our drive for sex and that create the emotional bonds which help with raising a family.

However, we have also been divided into male and female, and, though we have the same long-term goals in mind, our individual approaches are very different. There lie the inherent stresses of being human. Along with money, love and sex are the focus of a large part of our mental time and energy. Is he or she "the one"? When am I going to see him or her again? Should I stay? Should I go? It can be emotional roller coaster.

Night work can help smooth out this drama without taking away the potential for its ecstasy. It can lift you out of emotional ruts and repetitive thinking patterns that paralyze you, freeing you to feel you've done something to move the situation forward and get on with your day. That said, there are a few very important rules when handling relationships, especially in the realm we travel on our night journeys - the realm of the subconscious.

AVOIDING MANIPULATION

As I mentioned in the safety chapter, and also especially important here: *everything* must be done "according to free will and for the highest good of all," which means no manipulation in any form. For instance, one form of manipulation is when you say to yourself, feeling justified and self-righteous: the person "should" do this or that. Or "I want them to do this or that" or behave in a certain way, or "get it" whatever "it" is. But this is just blaming someone else. And blaming someone else doesn't fix anything. It just creates a burden of anger that will make you sick in the long run. So it is not about changing the other person. It's about changing yourself and addressing the connection between the two of you.

It's not about how they think of you or act toward you. It's about how you feel about yourself first. Then it's about healing the space between you. Think of the old saying that you will never know if you have someone's true affections unless you set him or her free. The goal is to create love and support around you, no matter who— love and support that is based on freedom and free will.

120

TRUSTING YOUR INNER WISDOM

As an intuitive healer, I have learned that my work is best when I set my intention as a healer, clear my mind and then blend gently into the client's system and energies. I then ask and allow his or her inner wisdom to show me their optimal path of healing. I am often amazed at what my clients will offer as solutions and I truly enjoy following their lead through the twists and turns of their unwinding because I know that the solutions they show me are far more brilliant than anything I would have imagined, and far more effective on many levels. When I was trained in this type of healing, I was told that if, in my thinking mind, I decided what I thought was good for a person on a whole, soul level, that 99.99 percent of the time, I would be wrong. That means that after I diagnose and treat on a purely physical level, I treat on a soul level and support the soul in unveiling its own perfect solution. It's a relief to know that somewhere in our minds and wisdom lies the perfect solution to every dilemma, every setback, and every relationship.

JOURNEYS TO LOVE

The following phrases of love will take you deep within, then far into the universe. When you return, having touched these places, you will have a perspective on love that will create a beautiful foundation for your life and your world. Then ice this cake with poetry, tenderness and fun and share it with someone special!

Check the weather, make sure your ship is ship-shape and put on your captain's uniform:

In Love and Light
According to Free Will and for the Good of All
For My Highest and Best Good
I call forth in wholeness and harmony,
my authentic self, my inner wisdom and my diving essence.

Invite your crew as desired, then choose one phrase to learn:

Please teach me how to love myself completely

Loving yourself completely is like cleaning your emotional house and filling it with beautiful personal decor.

Please teach me how to know who I am.

Knowing who you are creates a solid emotional center. It can be a long process of self-discovery, but it helps to prevent living your life for someone else, or living someone else's life for them. It promotes a sense of creativity and purpose

Please teach me how to feel loved by the universe

Feeling loved by the universe surrounds you with external support. This frees you from the tendency to depend on one or a few people for this support. Creating a sense of external spiritual support is the goal of many religions. However it is my belief that loving support must begin within with self-love, and be balanced by the receiving of love reflected, amplified and returned back to you by the great mirror of the universe.

Please teach me how it feels to create love.

Creating love from within balances the external and internal flow of love and support. If you nurture this ability to create love from your heart center and shine it outward, it can give a profound sense of balance and power to your place in the universe. You become creator as well as created and stand as an equal in company with all the loving spiritual leaders and guides whom you honor and respect.

Please teach me how it feels to know the Love and Support of the Universe through others in this world.

The universe loves and supports you from above, but it also loves and supports you from beneath your feet and through all life. It comes through the eyes of those you love and who love you.

Please teach me how to feel:
Beautiful, handsome, cherished, honored...

When you have created a foundation of love within and without, have fun with words, phrases and feelings that represent love in your everyday world. Feel the attractiveness that comes from an easy sense of enjoyment and creativity in life.

CAPTAIN'S LOG #6: A RELATIONSHIP WISH LIST

Someone once told me that if I wante to create an ideal relationship, I should make a list of at least 150 qualities which described the relationship that I wanted. This was to be an exhaustive list, covering every aspect of the relationship that I could think of. But then—and this was the challenge—I needed to *be* that list. I needed to find a way to feel and own those qualities within myself, because if I was out of harmony with my desires, they would never be able to come to me. If it actually showed up at my door,I wouldn't be able to accept it into my life.

Make that long list now. Then during your Magic Nights, ask for those qualities you think you may lack. It may take a long time to achieve some of them, but the journey itself will be full of its own magic.

WHAT YOU FOCUS ON EXPANDS

Another tool to support your efforts on a mental and subconscious level is to do some Feng Shui for your home and your life that will enhance and create fertile ground for your vision. Create a setting that invites what you want into your life. Do the things that invite the scenario that you dream of. Do what makes you feel loved and alive. Arrange things in pairs if you want to attract a relationship. Surround yourself with images and input that support what you want to create. Example: choose a love game instead of a war game. Choose a TV show that has some good romantic characters and creates good feelings about other people. Choose cooperation and forward motion over conflict and decline. What you focus on expands, and if you focus on negative situations and images, they will occupy your mind and your dreams and become your life. Take the blinders off and focus on that which feeds you, makes you feel how you want to feel.

In the end, it's not what you're doing that attracts. It's who you are and how you feel about yourself and life. Create your feelings of success and joy in life in the way you choose. Radiate them with confidence and ease. Smile and the world will smile with you.

ITINERARY #5: HAPPY, HEALTHY, BUSY AND CREATIVE
Some Magic Words to create attractivesness are:

Please teach me how it feels in every aspect of my being and every area of my life to be happy, healthy, busy and creative, in all the ways that are for my highest and best good and are for the highest good of all.

TWO CIRCLES, TWO SHIPS

Another way I have found to create positive harmonious transformation in any relationship is by creating two circles. In your mind, invite and circle all of your helpers, healers, and guides around you. Then envision the person you wish to heal your relationship with and invite all of their helpers, healers, and guides to encircle them. Place the circles so that their perimeters just touch. Then invite your respective helpers healers and guides to heal, harmonize and balance the energy between you. Relax, watch and feel your guides get to work. Stay focused and relaxed until you feel finished, complete and at peace.

Continue this vision on your night's journey. Go out with two ships, yours and theirs. Set the destination to wherever is the best healing, harmonious, loving and lovely place you both could possibly go, to heal your relationship to yourself, and to heal the space between you.

BEAUTIFUL

Is there some negative idea or belief that you have about yourself that seems so deep-seated that no matter what you do, it keeps seeping to the surface? Do you say to others, "I'm just not lucky" or "Life is hard"?

One such belief I had was that I was ugly. I remember my brother telling me I was ugly when I was very small and it was a well-known fact in our family that my older sister was the "pretty girl," which meant I must not have been pretty. Apparently I was a late bloomer. When I told people as a young adult about that belief in my fundamental ugliness, they simply looked astonished. Not that I was a stunning beauty, but I was at least attractive. However, I had discovered through years of therapeutic adventures that this belief that I was ugly was very deeply rooted in my subconscious.

127

Once, as a gift to myself, I committed to an entire year of discovering, feeling and knowing my true beauty. For that year, I asked the universe:

Please teach me how it feels to be beautiful, on all levels and aspects of my being, in past, present and future, in all time and space.

After one year, I felt better about my self-image. However, as I get older I revisit my self-image from time to time and find new levels and aspects of beauty to feel and enjoy. Someone asked me the other day how I envisioned myself in the future. I replied that I saw myself as a rich (fun) old lady who wore too much lipstick, and I laughed.

A JOURNEY TO HEAL, LOVE AND THE VISION THAT FOLLOWED

When I began experimenting with my Magic Nights, I used these journeys to work toward healing my relationship with and old flame from college. I hadn't seen or been in contact with him in many years, but despite all my best efforts I was unable to forget about him completely. Every now and then his essence would bubble up from some place deep within me and I would be thrown off course romantically once again. It just wasn't healthy. I wanted to move to the next place, take the next step forward to freedom for both of us. Once, when my thoughts wandered to him, my guidance told me to ask him why he was there. What was his purpose for being there still, deep within me?

So I got on my ship at night, invited my crew and invited his higher self, his authentic self, his divine nature to come aboard. I set the intention for our highest good and fell asleep. In the morning, I envisioned myself back on the deck of my ship and reconnected with everyone there. I sat down across from him and asked him.

"Why are you still here inside me?"

He stared at me silently, but visions began to come into my mind. It's a past life. I am a woman in Scotland in the fourteenth century. I am grieving, kneeling beside a small, shallow grave I have dug with my own hands. I clutch my stillborn baby girl to my chest. (I understood that this child had contained his spirit. Was I Catholic? Did she die without being baptized? Do I feel guilt as well?) I hear myself promising to always hold her in my heart, to never to let her go. I promise, I *vow*... *(*Uh-oh. That vow was heartfelt and deep. I guess I never really did let her go.)

Whether these visions are historically accurate was not important. What was important is that, no matter what form it took, I was being given another opportunity to heal something between us, and I took it. As I have done in the past, I decided to go back into that vision and be with my past-life self as a kind of guardian angel from the future. I called forth my authentic self, my divine presence and my inner wisdom; I put on my best angel costume and went to her.

An angelic feeling came over me. The costume was working well. I comforted her, and then I spoke to her slowly, allowing each phrase to sink in:

"To remember love is a divine thing,
To respect the living compassionate,
To honor yourself a matter of survival.
Honor your path
Honor your destiny
Honor the love that created you
And you have Heaven on Earth

Give yourself to her as she has given herself to you.
Open your heart and receive all the love that is offered.

129

It is your destiny
To love and be loved
To heal and be healed
To dance with joy with the stars, the moon and the sun.

To love and be loved.
To handle the earth with care.
To walk upon her softly,
Sing with her her song,
Be gentle with her creatures.

It is love that heals the wounds
And finds the joy in another day,
Another dance,
Another breath of peace within the world.

Love yourself as you have loved no other.
For it is that love which frees you
And finds you as you are
A blessed one, divine goddess amongst the stars
Beautiful lady, be as you are. Be at peace.
For I am with you always."

I stayed with her a little while longer, until she was peaceful. Then I came back to this world and this place, feeling incredibly blessed at all I had just experienced and felt. This was the answer to my question. What do I know about love? I know that I love, and I am loved. That is all I need to know.

TREASURE

Treasure: that mythical image of a wooden box overflowing with gold and jewels. Though it has been very real in days gone by, it has left us with only tantalizing glimpses of its glory—coins unearthed from just beneath the gentle soil of farmland and sunken ships buried in the sand beneath the waves.

The treasure of the past is hard, gold, glorious, dangerous, and exciting, but the treasure of now is buried deep within each of us and the adventure of its discovery is no less treacherous. We must overcome the powerful waves of our fears, new and old. We must battle our most fortified inner defenses. We must fearlessly dive deep within our souls. This treasure that is uniquely our own is there, waiting for us to touch its heavy wooden lid and lift the latch.

When I put my hands on my clients, I search for that treasure because I have found, again and again, that when I release restrictions and old pain patterns, it's like lifting the lid of a treasure chest. There is always a bright glimpse of talent and potential

131

hidden underneath that heavy lid. I have never found the treasure chest to be empty. Every one of us has untapped and unearthed potential. We can all be more and have more and enjoy more life than we understand in this moment. As a therapist, I take it as my mission to find and reveal the qualities, talents and potentials that lie hidden within each of us, buried beneath defensive walls of fear, anger, disappointment, and sadness.

Because what we focus on expands in life, I choose to focus on the potential within that treasure chest. The aches, pains, and frustrations that we have are like stones, dirt, sand, logs, heavy chains, and anchors that hold us down, keeping us back from our true potential and preventing us from expressing those qualities within that are our treasures and our gifts to ourselves and the world. With myself and my clients, I carefully breach those walls, lift those logs and unlock those shackles, and with each release, a new treasure is revealed.

When I discovered the deeply buried treasure chest within my own body, I made sure to feel the treasure-ness of it as fully as I was able to in that moment. And now that I have had a taste of that feeling, I can use the magic words and mentally touch that place within me again and again. I say, *"Please teach me how it feels to be a treasure."* I now understand that I am the treasure I seek.

Some people are considered treasures in their own families, their towns, or even their countries. Like movie stars or world leaders, some people are treasured by people all over the world. They seem to express from every atom of their body the feeling of a treasure chest that is overflowing. People naturally surround them and follow them wherever they go, picking up the stray coins that spill over the rim and litter the ground around them. How are you a treasure?

ITINERARY #6: YOU ARE THE TREASURE

How are you a treasure? What is your gift to your family? Your community? The world? Just ask for your Magic Nights Journeys to:

Please teach me how it feels to be a treasure.

You are the treasure you seek.

CAPTAIN'S EPILOGUE

The world around us is changing very quickly. It is time to feel the joy and gifts of our treasures as we come together and share them with each other. It is time to create the fabric of a new world before the fabric of the old world fails completely. It is becoming apparent that the stresses on our planet and our social structures threaten our very survival as a species. There is a sense of urgency. Change needs to happen quickly. We need to change and become more than we thought possible. We have a choice to make. Do we leave our treasures safely buried and go down the road to an apocalypse, or pull up our bootstraps very quickly, use our intuition, innovation and the creation of a new sense of community to find new and better solutions?

"...Perhaps the evolution of intelligence in Man can be answered in broad terms by "Emergence" Theory. Science explains that emergence is when something interesting emerges when it would not normally be expected to do so. For example, the formation of stars and planets from atoms, the way a flock of birds will all fly and turn in unison, and even life itself.

The most interesting thing about emergence is its inevitability. It's like a pre-programmed sequence of events that inevitably lead to the formation of everything we see, to life and possibly even to the development of our intelligence. I think the science for this is still in its early stages, but it is a fascinating concept..." Andrew Canterbury, UK on 8/11/2010 in response to a Mail Online article: "Home Sweet Stone-age Home" by David Derbyshire

What are we emerging into? How are we evolving? Perhaps work like *Magic Nights* is part of that equation. Perhaps it's a way of exercising those brain muscles that have become lax, reigniting any deactivated DNA that might be hanging around and pushing our evolutionary potential to the max.

Thankfully, at least in my experience, it seems like we have a lot of help—a big extraterrestrial and etheric cheering section waiting on the sidelines to coach us and help us be the best we can be—but, ultimately, it's up to us to work night and day for solutions.

It's my fondest hope that this night work can be another tool in our bid for survival as a species, that we can reach far and wide into the unknown, into the vast potential of the universe within and without and find the answers we so desperately need. I'm going to ride that wave and sail those seas and dream a new dream. I'd love to see you there beside me.

SHIP'S LIBRARY

LINKS TO TEACHERS AND FRIENDS

Abraham, Esther and Jerry Hicks, who teach the power of emotion. - www.abraham-hicks.com

Armor Keller, my fabulous friend and artist who shared her gifts for this work. - www.armorkeller.com

The Divine Creatives Group: My publishing website and links to my work and world. - www.divinecreativesgroup.com

The Foundation for Shamanic Studies: The organization that offered spiritual structure when I needed it. - www.shamanism.org

Sondra Ray, the fabulous teacher of Unlimited Life and Loving Relationships. - www.sondraray.com

Dr. John Upledger, honored mentor and teacher of CranioSacral Therapy - www.upledger.com

CPSIA information can be obtained at www.ICGtesting.com
Printed in the USA
BVOW02s0201071013

333071BV00001B/15/P

9 780615 442129